The Har

Tom McGrath 1940 – 2009

Tom McGrath was born in Rutherglen, Scotland, in 1940, Tom McGrath was a poet, journalist and musician. Beginning with his plays *Laurel and Hardy* (1976) and *The Hard Man* (1977) which he co-wrote with Jimmy Boyle, his popularity and reputation as a playwright became international. *The Dream Train* (written for Magnetic North Theatre Company) was read in French translation at the Avignon Theatre Festival (2001) and produced in Finland and in Germany. A gifted pianist, he was musical director on Billy Connolly and Tom Buchan's *The Great Northern Welly Boot Show* (1972), a riotous celebration of the Upper Clyde ship-builders' work-in. Two years later, having already brought Miles Davis, Duke Ellington and the Mahavishnu Orchestra to Glasgow, he set up the Third Eye Centre, a shrine to the avant garde, which is still in operation as the Centre for Contemporary Arts. By the time he left in 1977, he was establishing his name as a playwright with close ties to Edinburgh's Traverse, but also found time to establish Glasgow's Tron Theatre at the turn of the decade. In 1979 he wrote *Animal*, which consists almost entirely of stage directions and the grunts of apes. His other plays include *The Android Circuit*, *1-2-3* and *Buchanan* as well as a modern version of *Electra* and a two-part adaptation of Tankred Dorst's *Merlin* – translated by Ella Wildridge, his partner of twenty years. His last play was *My Old Man*. As important as these was his work supporting a generation of playwrights – among them David Harrower, David Greig and Douglas Maxwell and it is thanks to McGrath that the Playwrights' Studio, Scotland was established in 2004.

Jimmy Boyle

Jimmy Boyle was born in Gorbals, Glasgow in 1944 and is a Scottish sculptor and novelist who was formerly a gangster. In 1967 he was sentenced to life imprisonment for the murder of another gangland figure, William 'Babs' Rooney, although Boyle denies that he committed this killing. During his imprisonment in the special unit of Barlinnie Prison, he turned to art and wrote an autobiography, *A Sense of Freedom* (1977), which has since been filmed. On his release from prison he married psychotherapist Sarah Juliet Trevelyan and moved to Edinburgh to continue his artistic career. He designed the largest concrete sculpture in Europe, *Gulliver* for The Craigmillar Festival Society in 1976. The following year he co-wrote the play *The Hard Man* with Tom McGrath which premiered at the Traverse Theatre in 1977. Boyle has also published *Pain of Confinement: Prison Diaries* (1984), and a novel, *Hero of the Underworld* (1999). The latter was adapted for a French film, *La Rage et le Reve des Condamnes (The Anger and Dreams of the Condemned)*, and won the best documentary prize at the FIFA Montreal awards in 2002. He now lives and works in France and Morocco with his second wife, Kate Fenwick.

fairplay press

The Hard Man

by Tom McGrath
and Jimmy Boyle

fairplay press

First published in 1977 by Cannongate and this edition published by fairplay press, an imprint of Capercaillie Books Limited in 2011.

Registered office 1 Rutland Court, Edinburgh.

Printed in the UK by CPI Bookmarque, Croydon

A catalogue record for this book is available from the British Library.

ISBN 978-1-906220-41-9

Introduction to 2011 edition

After the huge and unexpected success of his first play, *Laurel and Hardy* in 1976, Glasgow playwright Tom McGrath was asked by the Traverse Theatre what his next play would be. 'It's going to be about violence' he said. He was asked for a title; he quickly made one up. 'It's going to be called *The Hard Man*'. McGrath was concerned with his home city's fetishisation of violence, and its prevalence in its working class culture. He had become fascinated by the violence in the work of Laurel and Hardy and began to imagine what the films would be like without the laughs. Or only with the violence.

As he worked away on ideas and sketches for his new play, he began an extraordinary correspondence with one of Scotland's most notorious hard men, Jimmy Boyle. Boyle was an inmate at the special unit at Barlinne prison, serving a life sentence for murder; a crime he claimed he did not commit. The correspondence between the two formed the basis of the powerful and influential play-cum-bloody cabaret *The Hard Man*. It changed the life of McGrath and the face of Scottish theatre. It was the *Black Watch* of its day. It was popular, challenging and contemporary. It was a theatrical game-changer. Imagine *Scum*, meets *The Threepenny Opera*, meets *Goodfellas* staged in a music hall and underscored by Charlie Mingus. It's got the heart of *Men Should Weep* with the soul of Allen Ginsberg and the hairstyle of Jonny Rotten. It paved the way for *Trainspotting*, and shares a purpose with Sarah Kane.

The story is a fictionalised account of Boyle's young life. From his days as petty criminal, through numerous stretches in brutal young offenders units, in to organized crime, money lending rackets, notoriety, arrest, imprisonment, more brutalization and a bloody *battle-royale* with the prison guards at HMP Peterhead. The play was derided in some quarters for adding lustre to the reputation of a violent criminal and convicted murderer. For others the play represented an attack on the corrosive influence of gang-culture. For others it was a poetic meditation on state violence and the question of who is criminalized and how they are punished. For others the play represented the rage of the indefatigable human spirit against the madness of the system – a Gorbals *One Flew Over The Cuckoos Nest*. The politics of the play continue to be provocative in their ambiguity.

The play is complex, stylised and difficult to pin down; but it reflects the truth of our protagonist's 'version of his own story' on a deeper level. It's expressionistic, it seizes the essence of life without its context; as Tennesse Williams said of his own expressionism 'it's a closer approach to truth'. Its structure owes a lot to McGrath's love of jazz, it freewheels like a Charlie Parker sax solo, but always returns effortlessly to the main theme. Its demotic language is rich with turns of phrase recalled from Boyle's childhood in the Gorbals. The synthesis of the two gives us a play of startling originality.

When I first read *The Hard Man* two and a half years ago, I was swept up in its energy, frankness and jet black working class wit. It's zoetrope of violent imagery lodged in my brain like splinters of glass. It appealed to the adolescent in me that loves gangster films, the child that loves pantomimes, and laughing at dirty jokes. It appealed to the part of me that is curious to know why we are fascinated with violence and its perpetrators; the part that is riveted by *Silent Witness* and *Macbeth*. The part of me that questions why I can check my phone while watching far off cities get bombed on the news.

The more I read it, the more I felt that 2011 was a fecund time to explore the play. The end of 2010 saw Manchester United's Rio Ferdinand campaigning for action to stop kids killing each other with knives in Peckham and the strangling of a young woman in Bristol. It saw *Wikileaks* reveal how British prisoner abuses at Abu-Ghraib has led to the radicalization of thousands of young Iraqi men, creating a foothold for Al-Qaeda where there was none. It saw millions being paid in compensation to former inmates of Guantanamo Bay. In each case 'them', 'the others' suddenly became people who had names and feelings and spoke on Newsnight. Johnny Byrne's sardonic spoken leitmotif 'the animal is thinking', had an increasingly sonorous resonance.

There is a theme of debt in the play too, which felt deeply contemporary. This is expressed on a figurative and moral level, as the actors who play the characters that Byrne betrays in act one return in the guise of his jailers and tormentors in act two. But the issue of working class debt and the problem of what happens when people have no-recourse to 'legitimate' credit is tackled head on also. Johnny Byrne says

'I was providing a social service . . . I'd been prepared to do business with them when you hadn't. While you were sitting back pretending not to notice I had been there to care for their needs. My methods with defaulters were quick and to the point but they weren't any different from your precious world just a bit less hypocritical and undisguised. Let's face it the whole world is a money lending racket and if it takes a man's whole life to kill him with his debts it doesn't make it any the less an act of murder'

The juxtaposition of moral law with written law and the troubling gap between the two is of profound interest to McGrath and Boyle. As is the issue of who society deems to be 'criminal'. It was perfectly legal for banks to sell mortgages to people who couldn't afford to pay them back. The illegal sale of toxic debt remains largely unpunished. Bankers continue to receive their bonuses, and the banks are bailed out to the tune of thirteen trillion dollars in the US and counting. Tony Blair started what many believe to be an illegal war and gets £1million per gig, speaking on leadership. Brutal prisons the world over, are crammed with the mentally ill and addicts of all kinds who do not have powerful friends, or happen to disagree with their government, or who had the misfortune to deal in sums society could comprehend.

The British government attempted to have Jimmy Boyle sentenced to hang in 1967 for a murder charge that was eventually thrown out of court. His actions in prison, as far as he was concerned, were purely a practical matter of surviving the actions of a state that had physically and sexually assaulted him in his teens and at the age of twenty-three tried to rush through a flawed conviction that would have seen him dead. However the shadow of Jimmy Boyle doesn't loom as large over the play as it did in 1977. Maybe we are more able, with distance, to dispassionately consider the fictional character of Johnny Byrne and hear the play's jagged poetic rhythms and its passionate polemic on its own terms.

The play doesn't say that Byrne is innocent or even that he is good, just that he is man who was brutalized, who brutalized others, who in turn brutalized him. To what extent he is a hero and to what extent he is a bastard is entirely up to you. He was reduced to the status of an animal, living in a cage, caked in his own shit. We know that after the shocking final moments of the play, given the opportunity, the real life 'animal' was able to change his circumstances. Although the special unit that did so much to change Boyle's life was closed down in 1994. Between 1996 and 1998 eight inmates committed suicide.

The play reminds the audience that arguments about the punishment of criminals are general and abstract when applied to other people, but very specific when applied to you. It's fine to punish 'them', 'they' deserve it, 'they' have broken the law, 'they' deserve everything that's coming to them. 'They' have a name. 'They' are not going to disappear.

Phillip Breen 2010, Director of the 2011 production

Thoughts on the first production

I met Jimmy Boyle for the first and only time while he was in Barlinnie Prison's Special Unit, an experiment in prisoner rehabilitation. Tom McGrath and I sat on his bed, Boyle came in and closed the door behind him. That was interesting and unexpected: a prisoner deliberately locking himself and us in. He positioned himself on the opposite wall where he could see both of us and the door at the same time. Tom and he spoke intently about the play. I wanted to get a sense of what kind of 'animal' he was. That's how he was popularly known. He never looked us in the eyes once, his gaze was always to the door. Boyle was very fit, and febrile. I came away feeling there was social ineptitude, something that wasn't but should be there in his social make-up. Nonetheless, when it came time to go Boyle wished the production well – its success might help get release. He trusted me to deliver his typewritten manuscript of *A Sense of Freedom* to Canongate publishers in Edinburgh, which I duly did.

I didn't appreciate just how notorious Boyle was, and that everybody in Scotland seemed to hold strong opinions about him. As soon as rehearsals began in the spring of 1977 the press was snooping around. Even the tabloids. Newspapers began saying that we were letting ourselves be duped, that Boyle was going over the head of the prison system and appealing directly to the people, 'he was scum'. The cast consisted of Martin Black, Michael Carter, Ian (a.k.a. Kenny) Ireland, Peter Kelly, Frances Low, Ann Scott-Jones, Benny Young – with Ronnie Goodman on percussion. All of us were passionate about the play, and everybody helped make the production what it became. The whole production began to take on a life of its own. Newspaper pressure was seeping through into rehearsals. There was no avoiding our production of *The Hardman* was becoming controversial.

Rehearsals were held in a fog of cigarette smoke. Much of rehearsals were spent finding ever new ways of staging violence. There was so much in the script and Boyle's story. We explored how to develop violence through engaging with the energies and rhythms of our bodies, in the language, and we spent a lot of time choreographing each moment. We did good work. Getting there was hard. But the violence we were exploring was beginning to seep into our relationships with each other. We had arguments, were short tempered, shouted at each other, and on edge and just had to find more energy to do the production. At the end of days we all went our separate ways. We had to have space from each other.

We started running *The Hardman*. The first half became movement violence sound – a high octane dance. The story telling was bursting through the Traverse walls. We opened. The appropriateness of giving Boyle publicity through this production was conflated with the production itself. Reviews were mixed. Many thought the

5

production romanticized Boyle. It didn't seem to matter what newspapers said, the audiences wanted to know more about him. They loved the physicality of our production, and the run easily sold out.

The Hardman then took on a life of its own. Towards the end of 1977 we toured to London and early in 1978 we did a seven week tour of England, and were part of the Traverse's 1978 Festival season. It was then revived again and played at The Pavilion Theatre in Glasgow (we transferred from our 100 to a 1449 seat theatre) before going to the Kammerspiele in Munich.

As I write this, I'm wondering how it will play today? I'm intrigued. Scotland is such a different place now – there have been so many changes. In 1976 Boyle was still in prison. There was no guarantee he was ever going to be released anytime soon. The tabloids were intent on making sure he stayed in prison. And part of the controversy of our production lay in that unresolved tension. The Traverse then self-consciously did plays by new Scottish writers, and I'm pleased that plays such as *The Hardman* form part of Scotland's confident cultural past.

In part I hope this production also remembers Tom McGrath. Even after these many years I still know what his presence feels like. I was so sad when he died last year. My first impression of him was a laughing Bhudda. He was funny, smart, at times cantankerous, very generous to me, sometimes, always full of ideas, poetry, stories. There was such energy and rich thinking around him.

Peter Lichtenfels, January 2011

Characters

JOHNNY BYRNE:	Glaswegian gangster
SLUGGER	
BANDIT	
DEADEYE	His associates
BIG DANNY	
ARCHIE	
KELLY	Victims of assault
CAROLE:	BYRNE'S girlfriend
MAW:	BYRNE'S mother
LIZZIE	
MAGGIE	Two gossips
DIDI:	Prostitute
LEWIS:	BYRNE's lawyer
MOCHAN:	Prisoner
COMMANDO:	The Assistant Governor of the Prison
JOHNSTONE	
PAISLEY	Prison officers
RENFREW	
POLICEMAN	
CLERK OF COURT	
WOMAN WITH ARCHIE	
BAR WOMAN	
PERCUSSIONIST	

Setting

The action is set in a variety of locations on Clydeside and in Scottish prisons.

Act 1

Lights come down. Darkness. Fragment of a song:

Oh the River Clyde's a wonderful sight,
the name of it thrills me and fills me with pride.
Oh I'm satisfied whate'er may betide,
the Sweetest of Songs is the Song of the Clyde.

Lights come up on the windae-hingers – two women, LIZZIE and MAGGIE, leaning out of their tenement house windows. They have their elbows on the window-ledge and are having a conversation across the street.

LIZZIE: Hullo, Maggie.

MAGGIE: Hullo there, Lizzie.

LIZZIE: Maggie, where did your man come frae?

MAGGIE: Seymour Street. Ah hear its getting awfae bad up there. Ah think we just moved oot in time.

LIZZIE: Yir no kiddin. Thir wus a man kilt up thair the other night. The Spaniard. Did you know him?

MAGGIE: Oh aye. McTaggart the Mad Spaniard. Everybody knew him. He wus a right bad loat. Ah might've known he'd come tae a sticky end. Whit happened tae him enyway?

LIZZIE: He wus laying oan the street in Maryhill Road – just ootside the HLI pub fur oors an' oors. We wur oan the buses, oan the night-service, an' we saw him laying there up an' doon fur aboot four journies. Even from the bus in the dark you could see the blood. They say they put the knife in at the bottom of his stomach and ripped him open.

MAGGIE: Did the polis no dae anythin aboot it?

9

LIZZIE: Naw, Thae jist let him lie thair. They wur glad tae be rid o him.

MAGGIE: And did they no get anyone fur it?

LIZZIE: They never dae in gang fights, dae they? Oh but see efterwards, when they took the body away, we passed back doon oan the bus an aw you could see wus the chalk marks and the blood. And the Spaniard wusnae thair anymair . . .

Lights down. Windae-hingers withdraw.

BYRNE, SLUGGER and BANDIT rush on the stage in a state of alarm, looking behind them. They are obviously being pursued. BYRNE is alert but not afraid. They have stopped for a moment, breathless, looking back.

BANDIT: Oh my God! Oh . . . my . . . God!

BYRNE: **(Annoyed.)** Whit's the matter wae yae?

BANDIT: Whit dae you think?

SLUGGER: Aye. Naebody sed enythin aboot fuckin murder . . .

BYRNE: Ah didnae touch that mug.

BANDIT: No half yae didnae!

BYRNE: Listen, Bandit. You were in another room when it happened – enjoying the party – you never saw nothing. Same goes fur you, Slugger. You saw nothing neither. That mob will try tae put the finger oan me fur it, but ah didnae touch him. Huv you goat me?

SLUGGER: Goat yae.

BANDIT: **(More reluctantly.)** Goat yae.

BYRNE: **(Smiling, extending his open palm)** Right! Put it there, chinas! We're aw in it thegither! **(They both slap his out-stretched palm with their hands and say their line.)**

BANDIT: **(Slapping.)** We're aw in it thegither!

SLUGGER: **(Slapping.)** We're aw in it thegither!

BYRNE: O.K. Lets scarper. Different directions.

SLUGGER: See you doon the boozer.

BYRNE: Aye in aboot an oor's time. But go tae the other boozer, no the usual wan. They'll be looking fur us there . . .

Exit BANDIT and SLUGGER. Light change. BYRNE steps forward, looking around the audience.

BYRNE: My name is Byrne. Johnnie Byrne. I was born in the Gorbals District of Glasgow. You've read about me in the newspapers and heard about me in pubs. I'm a lunatic. A right bad lot. What the Judge always calls. 'A menace o society' I'm speaking to you tonight from a Scottish prison where I am serving life-sentence for murder. What you are going to see is my life as I remember it. What you are going to hear is my version of the story.

SLUGGER and BANDIT run on shouting.

SLUGGER: Rats.

BANDIT: Chasin' rats.

SLUGGER: Chasin' rats roon the backs.

BANDIT: Chasin' rats roon the backs wae a wee dug . . .

SLUGGER: Chasin' rats roon the backs wae a wee dug that wus rerr ut brekkin their necks.

BANDIT: It even goat a mention in the papers that wee dug, because it kilt that many rats.

SLUGGER: Hiya, Johnny.

BYRNE: Hiya, Slugger. Hiya, Bandit. Back tae school again . . . **(This line by way of explanation to audience.)**

SLUGGER: School! School! Back tae school. Ah hate a Monday.

BANDIT: Ah hate the fuckin' school. School's rubbish!

SLUGGER: Aye, whit's it aw aboot anyway? Who wants to learn aw that shite they teach yae?

BYRNE: You're that stupit, yae couldnae learn anythin anyway, even if yae wahntit tae.

SLUGGER: Listen to who's talkin. The teacher says you're a dead cert fur truble. He's goat you marked doon fur the Borstal already.

BYRNE: Fuck 'im.

BANDIT: Fancy doggin' it?

SLUGGER: Aye. Fancy it? We could go doon the shoaps an' dae some knockin'. Fancy it, Johnny?

BYRNE: Och, I don't know. We did that yesterday – and the day before. Ah think we're just wasin' oor time. Bars a chocolate an' boatles o scoosh. Ah wis aboot sick yesterday wae the amount ah ate.

BANDIT: Well, you were the wan that insistit oan goin' back tae the shoap an daein' it agen.

BYRNE: That wis just because ah wus bored. There's no much fun tae it wance you've done it a few times. An' enyway, its no bars o choclate we need, its money!

SLUGGER: Back tae that agen.

BANDIT: You bet your life its back tae that. Money. Lolly. Cash. It aw comes back tae that sooner or later, doesn't it?

BYRNE: Aye, well you know how we were talkin aboot daein a few shoaps at night?

BOTH: Aye.

BYRNE: An' we were tryin tae figure oot how we wid dae the loaks?

BOTH: Aye.

BYRNE: Well, I've been thinking . . .

BOTH: Miracles!

BYRNE: During the day, when they close up the shop for a coupla hours tae go hame an' huv a bit tae eat an' a wee snooze, maybe a pint doon ut the boozers . . . they cannae be bothered pittin aw thae loaks oan . . . its no worth it fur the shoart time thair oot . . . and enyway, they know that thieves only wurk ut night. . . . **(He smiles at them. They think about this.)** so . . . if we go during the day. . . .

SLUGGER: Goat ye.

BANDIT: Ya beauty.

BYRNE: So whit ur we waitin fur? Cumoan. **(To audience.)** I can't tell you about my chromosomes or genetic structure and I can't say anything about my Oedipus Complex or my Ego and my Id. Battered babies grow up to be people who batter babies. But I got nothing but affection when I was young – from my mother. My father – sometimes we wouldn't see him for days on end then he'd come home triumphant wae presents for everybody and half-bottle of whisky in, his back pocket.

One night he came home, lifted me up to the window, and said – 'Look down there, son. What do you see?' I saw a brand new, shining motorcar. 'It's all yours', he said. 'Tomorrow we'll go fur a hurl in it.' The next day I got up and looked out of the window. But the car was gone. And so was my father. And I never saw him again,

I remember my brothers and I at the funeral. There were four of us and we were sitting round the coffin, giggling. We wouldn't have laughed if we'd known what was coming.

SLUGGER and BANDIT run on, pretending to be kids in the street teasing BYRNE.

SLUGGER: Poorhoose! Poorhouse!

BANDIT: Look ut the Byrnes wae thir big broon suits an their tackety boots. Poorhoose! Poorhoose!

BYRNE: Him an' his brothers sleep four tae a bed!

BANDIT: Poorhoose! Poorhoose!

SLUGER: **(He and BANDIT are exiting as MOTHER enters.)** Their mammy's a skivvy fur the West End toafs.

BOTH: **(Exiting.)** Poorhoose! Poorhoose!

BYRNE and his MOTHER.

BYRNE: Hey Maw. Gonnae lend me half a knicker?

MAW: How? Where are you goin?

BYRNE: Ah'm goin oot wae the boys.

MAW: Where ti? Ah hope you're no going galavantin aw o'er the place and gettin intae trouble an' hiven the polis up at this door?

BYRNE: Ah'm no goin anywhere. Ah just want the money fur the pictures.

MAW: Ah've no goat that much. Here's a dollar, that'll huv tae dae yi. Be in here sharp the night. Ah've tae get up at five the morn.

BYRNE: You know ah'm always in early, Maw.

MAW: Aye. That'll be right. Aw ah know is yir always bringin the polis tae the door and givin that auld nosey bastard across the road somethin' tae talk about.

BYRNE: Don't worry aboot hur, Maw. She's been gossiping oot hur windae so long she's left hur diddie-marks oan the windae sill.

Exit BYRNE.

MAW: Right you. That's enough. Watch yir tongue. Mind and be in here early and nae fighting nor cerryin oan. **(To audience.)** Och, he wusnae a had boy really. It wus the company he kept. Ah could never believe aw the bad things people said aboot him, no even after he went tae prison. He wus ma son and he wus never any boather tae me. Ah mean, whit chance did he huv? He went alang tae the youth club an him an his mates were barred the very first night. Troublemakers! They were the very wans that needed some help. When he was younger, he wantit tae be an altar boy. But he wusnae allowed because he didnae huv any sandshoes – and ah couldnae afford tae buy him any. It wus oanly the toaffs that could afford tae kneel oan God's altar. Of course, toaffs tae us wur the people that lived jist up the street. In those days the television wus a new thing and it wus a great sign of wealth if yae hud a telly. We wur lucky if we hud enough tae keep us in food from day to day, nae wonder the boy turned tae thievin. He used tae come home wae presents fur me – things fur the hoose an' sometimes even a bit of money – and he'd pretend he'd worked fur thaim. Ah knew how he'd come by them and ah didnae like it and sometimes ah wid refuse his gifts. But maist o the time ah accepted – ah hud no option.

SLUGGER and BANDIT run on to the slage. MAW exits behind them.

SLUGGER: Nylons.

BANDIT: Bevvy.

SLUGGER: Trannies.

BANDIT: Dresses. We supplied the loat.

SLUGGER: The people couldnae afford tae buy things frae the shoaps –

BANDIT: It was a social service. **(Pointing to himself.)** To our society at any rate. It aw depends which side o the fence yir oan, doesn't it? Presents fur Christmas, a boatle fur Ne'erday, the orders wur always placed wae us. And Johnny Byrne became a popular young man about the Gorbals — a contact much sought after.

SLUGGER: While we made a foartune. Well, no much o a fortune but enough to keep us going for a while. For, after all, we were growing boys . . .

Enter DEADEYE and BYRNE from opposite sides of the stage. They walk straight into next scene which includes BANDIT and SLUGGER. DEADEYE speaks through his nose.

DEADEYE: Hello there, Johnny. Hiya, boys.

BOYS: **(Together.)** Hiya, Deadeye!

They do this greeting in style but DEADEYE is intent on his business with BYRNE. He is a small man in his forties. He goes straight to the point.

DEADEYE: Listen, Johnny, ah blagged some shirts there. Dae yae want tae buy any?

BYRNE: Let me see whit like they ur.

DEADEYE: Look at that. The best o' swag, Johnny, an' thair a real bargain so they urr.

BYRNE: How many huv yae goat?

DEADEYE: A gross. And ah'm puntin thaim cheap at a knicker each.

BYRNE: Och, cumon, Deadeye. Yir no trying tae punt thaim tae me at that price.

DEADEYE: Whit dae yae want? Dae yae want me tae throw thaim away? Yell no get shurts like that in the shoaps fur under a fiver.

BYRNE: Ah tell yae what, Deadeye. I'll give you half a knicker each fur thaim an' . . .

DEADEYE: Naw, naw . . .

BYRNE: . . . an' ah'll take the loat.

DEADEYE: The loat? A hale gross. You wid never get rid a them.

BYRNE: Let me worry aboot that. You take care a your end and ah'll take care of mine. Where ur the shurts? Doon ut the hoose? Right. Slugger, you go wae the wee yin an' pick up the rest a thaim. Ah'll settle up wae yae later, Deadeye.

Exit DEADEYE and SLUGGER. SLUGGER gently persuading DEADEYE on his way, DEADEYE a hit bemused by it all.

BYRNE: You take these doon tae Isaac the tailor and tell him he cun huv a groass a thaim ut Thirty Boab each.

BANDIT: Right-oh, Johnny.

Takes shirts and exits. BYRNE left alone on stage.

BYRNE: So we'd progressed. We'd started at the age of five, going round the doors collecting firewood and empty bottles, it was only a tiny step to stealing bars of chocolate, and a tiny step further to breaking locks and squeezing through windows. By this time I'd already done an Approved School stretch – for breaking into bubble gum machines, and I was beginning to get a sense of the way things are stacked. I cried my eyes out the night they took me away, pleaded with them and promised I would never do it again – it had only been a joke and I didn't feel I had done anything wrong but it was too late –

SLUGGER and BANDIT have re-entered.

SLUGGER: Alright, Byrne, stop dreaming. Strip. Wash. Scrub this in your hair, you little heap of vermin – grab hold of that bucket and *scrub that floor*!

BYRNE: But I scrubbed it yesterday and the day before.

SLUGGER: Well, scrub it again.

BANDIT: And don't but me, sonny, you're going to have to learn!

SLUGGER: That floor has been scrubbed a thousand times by boys like you down the years, and it'll be scrubbed a thousand times more, because, u know, its not the scrubbing that counts, not the sparkle off the floor, no its the lesson you learn while you're scrubbing.

BANDIT: And do you know what that is, Byrne? Or dae yae want us tae tell yae?

SLUGGER: Respect! Respect fur authority!

BANDIT: That's right. Respect fur authority. Authority. **(Brandishes cane.)** Authority.

They are circling him, threateningly. BANDIT has a cane. He becomes increasingly aroused.

SLUGGER: Authority and Private Property. **(Irish accent, Mimics priest. Makes blessing in the air.)** Blessed be Private Property Now and Forever Amen.

BANDIT: **(Almost diabolic. Thrashing with the cane in rhythm to the words.)**
Whack Whack Whack
On Your Bare Backside.
Just to make sure
You Don't Try it Again.

Gives a final whack and stands back. Breathless. Wipes his brow. SLUGGER takes on a mock air of schoolteacher. Produces a tawse from within his jacket and flexes it. BYRNE remains cowering back, his hands up to protect himself: SLUGGER speaks straight to the audience.

SLUGGER: Personally I prefer the tawse to the cane – flesh against flesh, it seems more humane.

BYRNE stands up slowly, with the bucket in his hand, carefully considering SLUGGER who is giving the audience a demonstration of how to use the tawse. BYRNE lifts the bucket and empties it over SLUGGER'S head. Slow blackout on SLUGGER dancing in rage with bucket on his head – BYRNE and BANDIT doubled up laughing.

Lights come back up on the windae-hingers, MAGGIE and LIZZIE.

MAGGIE: Howurr things, Lizzie?

LIZZIE: No bad. They could be better. Ma back's killin me an that doctoar doon the street's nae use at aw.

MAGGIE: Aye. Ah've changed away frae him. No so much because o him but o that bitch that cleans his office. Just because she writes oot his prescriptions fur him, she thinks she's a nurse.

LIZZIE: Aye, she bloody annoys me so she does, the way she struts aboot that surgery like the Queen o Sheba an' hur wae hur hoose like a midden an thae weans o hurs in a terrible state. She ought tae be ashamed o hursel.

MAGGIE: She hud the cheek tae tap a shilling aff o me fur the meter an ah huvnae seen her since. Ah'll be needin it back by Friday tae – ah need every penny!

LIZZIE: Ah'm in the same boat. Ah've goat the man comin in tae empty the meter this afternoon because ah need the rebate. Ah've nae money tae get the tea in fur him comin hame fae work.

MAGGIE: Ah'm expecting that H.P. man. Ah canna pay him this week an ah owe him six weeks awready.

LIZZIE: If ah see him comin ah'll send wan o the weans up tae shout through the letter box.

MAGGIE: Aye and let me know when he goes away cos the old bastard always stauns wae his ear ti the door listenin fur me . . .

They both withdraw. Enter BYRNE, SLUGGER and BANDIT. Rock beat from PERCUSSIONIST.

BANDIT: Johnny, the lads up in Shamrock Street wahnt us tae go o'er thair an' gie them haunders. There's a team comin doon frae the Caltan tae dae them over.

BYRNE: We're a thievin gang. We're no a fightin gang like thaim.

BANDIT: But they're just the next street, Johnny.

SLUGGER: Aye, and if we don't dae it, they'll say we crapped it.

BYRNE thinks it over.

BYRNE: Is there weapons?

BANDIT: That Calton team will huv bayonets and chains, boatles — the lot.

BYRNE: We better arm oorsels tae then.

BANDIT: Ah've goat a blade stashed away in the hoose.

SLUGGER: Wait till yae see the chib ah've goat. You'll never believe it.

SLUGGER and BANDIT stage a mock fight behind BYRNE as he speaks to audience. They have weapons and they stalk one another, leap on one another pretending to stab and hit.

BYRNE: Blades. Hammers. A splinter of glass. Anything did — just so long as it made a mark. A new dimension had entered my life. A new reality had opened up for me. Violence. It was inevitable.

Sometimes violence has a reason on the streets – its political, or religious, or a junkie killing for drugs – either a reason or an excuse. But in the world that I come from, violence is its own reason. Violence is an art form practised in and for itself. And you soon get to know your audience and what it is impresses them. You cut a man's face and somebody asks you, 'How many stitches?' 'Twenty' you say, and they look at you – 'Twenty? Only twenty? Christ, you hardly marked him.' The next time you cut a face you make a bit more certain it will be news.

He turns aside and doubles up holding his head. Rock beat. BANDIT and SLUGGER attend to him.

BYRNE: Ma heid! Ma heid! Ma fucking heid! The bastard kept hitting it wae a hammer.

BANDIT: Never mind, Johnny. You made a mess o him.

BYRNE: Ah wus so angry ah didnae know whit ah wus daein. He's no deid, is he?

BANDIT: He's no deid, but you just aboot gouged his eye oot wae that screwdriver you were carryin.

SLUGGER: They're aw saying yir crazy. They're sayin yir a lunatic. They're aw scairt tae fuck o yae.

BYRNE Straightens up and thinks this over. Smiles.

BYRNE: That's whit thair sayin is it? That ah'm a lunatic? That's awright then, isn't it? Ah ahm a lunatic. Ah'll dae anythin! You'se hud aw better watch it! **(They are afraid of him for a moment. He stretches out his palm as at beginning of play.)** Its just as well, eh? **(Smiling.)**

BANDIT: **(Smiling.)** Aye!

They slap hands. BANDIT and BYRNE, SLUGGER and BYRNE.

SLUGGER: **(Slapping.)** We're aw in it thegither.

They are laughing. BANDIT suddenly on the alert.

BANDIT: Hey, look. Here's Big Danny coming. Somebody said he hud a joab fur you, Johnny, doon at his shebeen.

SLUGGER: Yir going places, Johnny.

LIZZIE: **(Looking out of her window.)** Johnny, you're a mug!

BYRNE looks at her questioningly. Rock beat. Enter BIG DANNY.

BANDIT: **(With a flourish.)** Big Danny!

SLUGGER: Look at the suit! Get the material!

DANNY is in his late forties. A flashy suit and tie, well-pleased with himself. Smoking a cigar.

DANNY: **(To audience.)** They call me Big Danny and ah run a shebeen. Dae yae's all know what a shebeen is? Well, its like Prohibition but its no as big. In Glasgow, when these boys were still boys — before thae goat too big fur their boots — the pubs closed up at nine o'clock. Nine o'clock! Can you imagine it? So thir wur a loat o people wae drooths oan thaim aboot the town and it wus a simple matter, if yae wantit tae make some easy money, tae open up a wee place fur drinkin efter nine o'clock. And that's exactly whit ah did. Up a close in the Gorbals. A two room and kitchen. The place stacked wae bevvy. A shebeen! Ah wus in business — fur ma sell.

— Hullo there, boys. Howzit goin?

BYRNE: No bad, Danny. How's things wae you.

DANNY: Business is good, boys, but it could be better.

BANDIT: Whit dyae mean, Danny?

DANNY: **(Examining the tip of his cigar.)** Can ah ask youse boys a question?

BYRNE: Fire away.

DANNY: How much ur youse makin in a week frae yir thievin?

BYRNE: How much? I don't know, Danny. We don't really keep count.

DANNY Well, that's where youse ur makin a mistake because yae's should keep count. Let's face it, boys, none o youse ur ever gonnae work, ur yi?

BANDIT: Dead right we're no.

DANNY: Anyway, youse couldnae get a joab even if ye's wantit wan.

SLUGGER: Which we don't!

BYRNE: Ah hud a joab wance but it wus a waste o time, cooped up aw day wae somebody watching yir every move when yae could be oot oan the streets enjoyin yirsel . . .

DANNY: Aye. So whit else can ye dae but turn tae thievin. Yir hands are forced.

BANDIT: Nae option.

DANNY: A man's goat tae dae something tae keep himsel alive.

SLUGGER: An occupy his time . . .

DANNY: But wance ye've done that, yae've goat tae gie it some thoat. Wance a thief – always a thief. There's nae wae oot oh it. And yir maybe young now but youse'll soon be older.

BYRNE: Ah, come off it, Danny. Whit's aw this aboot?

SLUGGER: Aye, whit ur yae leading up tae, Danny?

DANNY: Oh, you'se ur clever boys alright. I can see that – except fur you, Byrne, everybudy knows you're a fuckin Hun. **(They all find this funny.)** so ah'll gie it tae ye's straight – how would youse boys like tae wurk fur me?

BANDIT: Wid we no just.

SLUGGER: Right an aw.

BYRNE: You two shut up and leave this to me. That wid depend. Danny.

DANNY: Whit wid it depend oan?

BYRNE: A loat o things.

DANNY: Like what?

BYRNE: Like what wid we be daein and whit wid you be payin us fur a start?

DANNY: Fur a start? Dae yae mean yae've goat mair conditions? Whit age ur you. Byrne?

BYRNE: Fourteen.

DANNY: Sweet Jesus, only fourteen and look ut him. Wahntin tae figure oot aw the angles before he's properly begun. Look, aw ahm lookin fur is somebody tae hang aboot in the streets at night ootside the shebeen tae bring the customers tae ma door. If youse boys urnae interested, ah can aye try somebody else.

BYRNE: Naebody else wurks in the streets in this part of town, and you know it.

BANDIT: Naebudy else wid dare.

BYRNE: Awright, so whit wid ye be payin us?

DANNY: Ah'm no sayin right now – but ah'll sae this, frae the look o you bunch an' the rags yir wearin, it'll be mair than yir making noo. **(BYRNE is annoyed by this. It looks for a moment as if there might be trouble.)** An' there's no point in lookin ut me like that, Byrne. Ah'm gieing yae a chance. Ah'm gieing yae a chance tae better yirsel. Because ah can see ye've goat – talent. What's your answer?

BYRNE: We'll need tae discuss it.

DANNY: Awright, discuss it then. Is it gonnae take long?

BYRNE: Naw. Just gie us a few minutes . . . **(Takes the others aside.)** Listen. don't let him see you're too keen. we've goat tae get as much oot oh this as . . . **(Conversation gets quieter as DANNY steps forward to talk to audience.)**

DANNY: Lamentable, isn't it? There ah was – wan big fool leading three young nitwits further intae the hole that he's in. You know what finally happened tae me? Ah didnae dae any big prison stretches, though ah wus in an oot the Bar-L same as the rest o them, but ah wus too weak tae be really crooked an ah took tae the boattle. If yae saw me nooadays it wid be oan a street coarner, wae stubble oan ma chin an ma clothes gone shabby – a hasbeen and a wino, gone beyond all hope. Ah didnae last long as bigshot . . . **(Returns to the boys.)** . . . so. Hus the great cooncil come to its decision. Whit a huddle. Youse ur wurse than the City fuckin Chambers.

BYRNE: We'll dae it – if the money's right.

DANNY: The money'll be right. Don't you worry about that. Comoan an ah'll get yies some chips tae celebrate.

SLUGGER: Tony the Tally wullnae let us in his chippy.

DANNY: He wull if ah tell him tae.

BANDIT: Good oan yae, Danny. Ah'll huv a fish supper.

SLUGGER: Ah wahnt a black puddin. Wae a pickled onion.

BYRNE: Could you get us in the pub. Danny?

DANNY: Johnny Byrne, now you're wae me, Big Danny, a loat o doors that previously were closed will suddenly magically be open tae yae.

BYRNE: Aye? That sounds fine.

Enter DANNY. He has a glass of whisky.

DANNY: Johnny, you an the boys huv been daein a loat o good wurk fur me.

BYRNE: Yae can say that again, Danny. When you took me oan ah didnae know ah'd be brekkin jaws fur yae.

DANNY: Well, in this game, Johnny, sometimes yae've goat tae be firm.

BYRNE: Aye, or get somebody else tae be firm fur ye.

DANNY: Whit ur you complainin aboot? Yir gettin paid well enough, urn't yae?

BYRNE: Aye. Fur the time being anyway.

DANNY: Naw, No just fur the time being. There's a bit mair action comin your way, Johnny. Ah wahnt tae make you ma right-hand man.

BYRNE: That's wise o you, Danny.

DANNY: Is that aw you've goat tae say. God, you're a close wee bugger. Two years yae've been workin fur me and you've always been so silent. But when you speak ah can feel the evil weighing down on your every word. Can ah trust yae, Johnny?

BYRNE: Whit's that yae've goat in yir hand, Danny?

DANNY: Bevvy. Whit does it look like?

BYRNE: Can yae trust the bevvy, Danny?

DANNY: You must be jokin. Ah see too much of it.

BYRNE: Well, if ye cannae trust yirsel wae the bevvy, yae cannae trust yirsel wae me. Because its no me or the bevvy you should be worryin aboot, it's yirsel . . .

DANNY: Aw, don't you worry about me. Ah'll see masell alright alright. Listen, did yae see that yin that owes me the hunner?

BYRNE: Aye, ah saw him.

DANNY: Whit did he huv tae say fur himsel?

BYRNE: He says his wife's pregnant and he's nae money. He says it'll take him another month or two.

DANNY: Whit did you say?

BYRNE: Ah said ah'd be back tae see him in a day or two.

DANNY: Did he get the message?

BYRNE: Whit dae you think?

DANNY: Aye. That's because he knows ah don't mess around. If he disnae come up wae the lolly . . . You get down and fix that fucker fur me.

BYRNE: Don't worry. Danny. Ah'll gie him a face like the map o Glasca.

Percussion. Rock rhythm. ARCHIE is rolling a cigarette. WOMAN is offstage.

WOMAN: Archie, are you no comm tae bed?

ARCHIE: Aye, ah'll be through in a minit, Jean. Just you go tae sleep.

WOMAN: Naw. Yae sat up aw last night, noo yir at it agen. An yae canny stay away fae that windae. Whit's the matter wae yae? Ur ye in some kind of trouble? Is there somebody efter yae?

ARCHIE: Naw, naw. Nuthin like that. Ah just cannae sleep these nights. Ah don't know whit it is. It must be wae the baby coming. Maybe I'm worrying.

WOMAN: I'd 've thought you'd be used to it by this time.

ARCHIE: **(To audience.)** When somebody's after you, you cannae sleep – unless you sleep wae one eye open. Every noise you hear from the street, could be the noise of him coming.

Footsteps on the pavement. A car draws up. The wind shakes and rattles at the window. Sometimes you wish he could come, just tae get it over with, just to put an end to this waiting.

WOMAN: Archie, are you coming tae bed or ur yae no?

Rock rhythms. DANNY and BYRNE.

DANNY: Noo that you've been upgraded, whit wid yae like?

BYRNE: **(To audience.)** So there I was standing with the sole of my shoe flapping, the buttons off my shirt and big holes all over my vest, and he's asking me what wid ah like. A right good suit with right good material, a brand spanking new white shirt and a tie to match. A pair of handmade shoes that were sparkling with polish. I always wanted to look like he does . . . **(To DANNY.)** I want a suit!

DANNY: A suit? Haw. Haw. I asked him what did he want and he said a suit! Awright, Johnny boy. First thing the morn's morn, downtae Isaac the Tailor . . .

They break and BYRNE stands to attention. Enter BANDIT and SLUGGER carrying suit.

WOMAN: **(She stands screaming at him.)** Monster! Sadistic bloody monster! You cut ma husband's face to shreds!

Drums. BYRNE is kitted out in suit. Eventually he stands resplendent.

LIZZIE: Yae never seen that fight last night, did yae?

MAGGIE: Naw. Ah didnae. But big Mary Boyce wus tellin me about it at the steamie this mornin.

LIZZIE: That Johnny Byrne half killed wan o those boys he wus fightin wae. Ah don't know how the poor soul managed tae pick hissel aff the ground the state he wis in.

MAGGIE: That's the thurd fight this week. It's time that Johnny Byrne grew up so it is.

LIZZIE: It's his maw ah feel sorry fur. She works aw day fur those boys so she does. She must be heartbroken.

MAGGIE: He's gonnae end up in Barlinnie the way he's goin. It's time he goat himsel a lassie an thoat aboot settlin doon.

LIZZIE: Aye. Aw him an his pals dae is sit in that pub aw day long drinkin an swearin, an that gaffer o the pub's just as bad because he gies thaim drink fur nuthin.

MAGGIE: He's just goan fae bad tae worse since he got in tow wae that Big Danny.

LIZZIE: That wee niaff!

MAGGIE: Ah think yir right. Lizzie. A lassie wid be the makins o that boy. Sometimes ah think its the only hope he's goat left.

Enter SLUGGER and BANDIT. BANDIT looking around him.

BANDIT: Is Johnny no here yet? Its no like him tae be late.

SLUGGER: He'll be wae the burd.

BANDIT: Aye, probably. **(Slightly derisive. Looks around him, taking in the audience.)** Thair they go, Slugger, the honest workin people. Whit a bunch o mugs They get up in the mornin and go oot tae wurk and get their miserable wages ut the end o the week tae help them pay fur their miserable wee hooses an' their miserable wee lives. Wance a year they're released fur two weeks. The Glesca Fair! An' thae aw go daft! Eejits! Two weeks later its back tae the grindstone again fur another year.

SLUGGER: Either that or they cannae get a joab an' they go aboot in fuckin poverty.

BANDIT: Well thank Christ that's no fur us. When we want something – we take it. And it doesnae matter who it belangs tae.

29

SLUGGER: When we take it, it belangs tae us.

BANDIT: Aye and aw the toffs and intellectuals hate oor guts. Because we're the wans that kick in thir doors an climb in thir windaes and run oaf wae aw their nice new presies an their family hierlooms. An they know we don't give a fuck. Efter we've done a place an left it in a mess, ah'll bet they can still feel us in the air roon aboot thaim an they wonder who we are. What we're like. Because its obvious we don't give a fuck . . .

SLUGGER: Smash their shoap windaes in. Dynamite their safes. Chib thaim in the street ut night an' run aff wae their money! Naw. They don't like us. They don't like us at aw.

BANDIT: An thae cun stuff their fuckin probation officers up thur fuckin arses. **(Pause.)** Here's Johnny coming. Aw naw, he's goat hur wae him.

Enter BYRNE and CAROLE. Talking and laughing. BANDIT interrupts them.

BANDIT: Hey, Johnny, fancy goin doon the Railway Club the night fur a bevvy?

CAROLE: I thought we were going out tonight.

BYRNE: Well, you can come alang wae us.

CAROLE: I thought we were going out by ourselves withoot thae two eejits.

Hits her.

BYRNE: Watchit, Carole. Ah've warned you before aboot cheekin me in front o the boys.

CAROLE: That's aw you worry aboot, isn't it? Yir reputation! Aw ahm good fur is cerryin yir chib an cop-watching fur yae.

BYRNE: Naw. That's no aw yir good fur.

CAROLE: Och, shut up you. You make me sick. Wan minit your aw affection, the next yir like a bluddy animal. You shouldnae tell me we're going oot if we're no.

SLUGGER: Oh, wid yae listen tae that. She'll be wahntin tae merry him next.

BYRNE: Right. Hurry up you if your comin.

CAROLE: Aw, piss off!

BYRNE Cumoan, lads.

BANDIT: Aye, furget, her, Johnny. Ah don't know whit yae see in hur.

BYRNE: Ah'm no asking you tae um ah?

BANDIT: Hey, fancy we'll go doon the Barrowland instead an pick up some burds.

SLUGGER: Nooky!

BYRNE: Aye, a fancy that. Haud oan. Hey, Carole, gie's ma chib.

CAROLE: Whit dae yae wahnt yir chib fur if yir just goin doon the Railway Club?

BYRNE: Never you mind. Just give us it an less o the questions. **(She gives it to him.)** Right. Ah'll see you later. Right, lads. Doon the Barraland. If any o that Calton mob jump us, we'll be ready for them.

SLUGGER: An ah thoat we wur going doon fur some nooky . . .

BANDIT: **(Triumphant.)** See yae later, Carole.

Exit BANDIT and SLUGGER. But BYRNE sits down behind CAROLE, with his back to her. CAROLE speaks to audience.

CAROLE: Later. Later. That's aw ah ever hear. Aw ahm good fur is keeping his chib an cop-watching fur him. Everybody says ah need ma heid looked going aboot wae him. He's a dead cert

31

road tae trouble, wan way or another. Ah'd like tae say that he was different when he wis wae me — quiet and gentle and affectionate like. But he's no. Ah suppose he must feel something for me — but if he does, he doesnae show it. Aw he's interestit in is his nookie then its doon tae the pub wae the boys.

BYRNE: Carole! Carole!

CAROLE: What's the matter?

BYRNE: Scratch ma back, Ah've goat a helluva itch.

CAROLE: Goad, yae never know the minit, dae yae? Whereaboots?

BYRNE: Just aboot there. That's it. Naw, a wee bit higher. Naw, lower. That's it. Oh, that's lovely . . . Rerr . . .

CAROLE: Here, leave me alane ya durty pig . . .

BYRNE: Stop it I like it . . .

CAROLE: Naw, really Ah've goat soup oan an ah doant want it tae overheat. It loses aw the flavour.

BYRNE: Oh well, you go right ahead wae yir soup, hen. Don't let me stoap yae. Yae'll make somebody a good wife wan o these days.

CAROLE: Aye well maybe one day yae'll huv tae marry me!

BYRNE: Och don't talk stupid!

CAROLE: Ah'm no talking stupid. Did naebday ever tell you the facts o life?

BYRNE: Ah mean whut dae yae wahnt tae be married tae a character like me fur? Ma roads mapped oot fur me. Ah keep a chib over the door an a blade in ma bedroom. That's when ahm no oan the run or oot causin damage. Ah'm for the Bar-L. It's inevitable.

CAROLE: It doesnae need tae be inevitable, Johnny. Yae can change things, you know.

BYRNE: Aw, gie us a brekk, wullyae? What can ah change? Fuck all.

CAROLE: Well, maybe if yae were married an hud a family . . .

BYRNE: Ah'd huv tae feed thaem. Or you'd huv tae feed them's mair likely. Just like my ma hud four o us tae feed efter ma father died.

CAROLE: But Johnny, even if yae did dae a stretch, you could rely oan me. Ah widnae mess yae aboot.

BYRNE: That's whit yae say now, but it's a different story when it happens. Look ut Big Jean – her husband's daein four years. She managed tae keep hursel fur him fur a year and that wus that. She started shacking up wae somebody else. Wait till he gets oot.

CAROLE: Ur you comparin me tae that Big Jean?

BYRNE: Naw ah'm no comparin yae tae . . .

CAROLE: It sounds very much tae me as if yae ur . . .

BYRNE: Aw in the name o . . . You know something, Carole?

CAROLE: What?

BYRNE: Ah'd love a plate o soup.

Rock rhythms.

Enter SLUGGER, speaks straight to audience.

SLUGGER: Ah wus up in Duke Street buying masel a coupla flash shurts an there wus a gemme oan ut Parkheid. The Old Firm. Jesus Christ, whit a bunch o eejits – grown men throwin screwtaps at each uther frae wan side o the road tae the uther, an aw in the name o religion. Ah don't know whit that's supposed tae be ahoot at aw. They wurk aw week then oan a Saturday thae go daft an split each other's heids open, then oan a Sunday thair oot tae twelve o'clock Mass un oan their knees. Sheer hypocrisy. **(Enter BANDIT.)**

BANDIT: Just so long as thair no taking money oot o oor pockets!

SLUGGER: Right an aw!

BYRNE: **(Approaching them.)** Aye, but you'll let Danny take money oot o your pockets.

BANDIT: Whit dae yae mean? It's Danny thut pays us, in' it?

BYRNE: Is it? So far as ah can see, we pay oorsels — underpay oorsels. Danny might hand over the notes tae us ut the end o the week, but that's aw he does. You think aboot it, when we startet wae Danny, we wur just boys. That wus two years ago. An Danny wis just runnin the Shebeen. It wus easy wurk. Noo he's intae everythin — every racket that's going, he's goat his finger in the pie. An' its us he's using tae dae it. He's goat us breakin jaws fur him an' taking aw the risks, but we're no seein enough return fur it personally.

BANDIT: So whit yae sayin? We'll chin him fur mair money?

BYRNE: Aye. Something like that.

BANDIT: Supposing he says no.

BYRNE: Whether Big Danny says yes or no makes no difference anymore.

BANDIT: I'm beginning tae see whit yae mean.

Enter DANNY.

DANNY: Hello there, boys, howzit goin? Still enjoyin the good life?

BYRNE: Hello, Danny.

BANDIT: Hello.

SLUGGER: Hello.

DANNY: Hey, whit's this? Aw the hellos. Ur you boys claimin me?

BANDIT: Yir gettin awfa sensitive in yir old age, Danny.

DANNY: Less o the old . . .

BYRNE: Its just that me an' the boys huv been discussin money.

DANNY: Ah should ah guessed. Well, ah suppose youse ur entitled tae a rise wae the way things ur expandin . . .

BYRNE: We don't want a rise, Danny.

DANNY: Whit dae yae want then?

BYRNE: We're intae yae fur the loat. **(Slashes him.)** We Rule, ya fool.

DANNY: O.K. . .

Percussion. Pub lights up. DEADEYE singing. Rock beat. DEADEYE's voice is heard in the darkness. LIGHTS come up on the domestic area. SLUGGER, BANDIT and BYRNE are seated, sharing a bottle of cheap wine with DEADEYE. Some of his swag is laying on the table. DEADEYE sings with his eyes closed, his arms outstretched. It is the Nat King Cole song *Too Young*.

DEADEYE: **(Singing.)** And yet we're not too young to know . . .
this love may last, though years may go . . .
and then some day they may recall . . .
we were not . . . too young . . . at all.

The boys laugh and cheer.

DEADEYE: **(Encouraged.)** I know a millionaire, who's burdened down with care.

BYRNE: **(Hastily interrupting him.)** Yir a good wee cunt, Deadeye, so yae urr.

DEADEYE: We're aw happy, int wi'? Ah mean we've aw earned a bit an' that's whit matters intit?

BYRNE: Mind any other swag yae get gie us a chance eh it first.

DEADEYE: Don't worry aboot that, Johnny. Ah know that if ah'm involved wae you an the mob, nae cunt's connae bump me fur ma money.

BANDIT: That's right, kiddo. An' you know none o us will bump yae.

DEADEYE: See that big bastard Ski doon ut the Bookies, he tried tae knock ma price doon ti fifteen bob by sayin' the material on the shirts wis shite. The big bastards worth a fortune as well.

BYRNE: Aye, he's a tight big bastard. Gie him nothin. He likes tae try and take liberties, an there's a loat o talk aboot him bein a grass.

BANDIT: Aye, that's right. He's supposed tae huv told the busies aboot wee Sniffer when he knocked him back fur some jewellery that he blagged.

BYRNE: Ah'll tell yae whit ah'll dae, Deadeye. Frae now on, don't bother dealing wae anybody else. Fae now on, any swag yi get gie me the chance o it and yae can put the word roon aw the young yins that urr blaggin swag an tell thaim that ah'll get thaim a good price fur it.

DEADEYE: Nae bother. Ah'll dae that. There's been too many cunts oot tae bump me recently.

SLUGGER: **(At a sign from BYRNE he is again bundling DEADEYE out.)** Just get the swag sent doon here an' we'll attend tae it.

DEADEYE: Right . . . Aye . . . **(Confused.)** Goodbye, Johnny.

BYRNE: Goodbye, Deadeye.

BANDIT: That's the right way. Johnny. Sew the whole district up. We can earn a right few quid if we get these guys in hand They blag some ace gear.

SLUGGER re-enters.

SLUGGER: Auld cunt. Ah thoat he'd never stoap talkin. He wus wahntin tae sing me another song oan the doorstep. Ah telt him tae wander.

BYRNE: Right. Slugger, sit doon. Ah wahnt tae talk tae yaes seriously fur a change.

SLUGGER: Its aboot money. People only talk serious when they're talking aboot money.

BYRNE: Cut it oot, Slugger. Right. Now look. Since we took over frae Big Danny we've taken over his contacts. We're intae everythin. The Docks. The Brasses. Protection. We've goat the loat. An' that's aw right as far as it goes, but ah think we cun take it further.

BANDIT: Never satisfied!

BYRNE: Sure ahm no satisfied. Because ah've come to realise somethin more and more strongly these days. We're no ut the thievin any more, we're runnin a business.

SLUGGER: You don't say. We'll need tae turn the shebeen intae an office then an pit oor names up on the door – J. Slugger, Company Secretary. Knock Three Times – Heavily.

BANDIT: Yeah an' we could get ourselves a nice little secretary with nice little tits and a waggly bum . . .

BYRNE: **(Laughing.)** Awright! Awright! Ya pair o eejits! Anyway, aw ahm leadin up tae the noo is tae say that ah wahnt us tae open a bank account.

SLUGGER: A bank account! Not on your Nellie! You'll huv us paying income tax next.

BYRNE: Naw. There's ways roon that. False credentials. You open an account in an assumed name.

SLUGGER: Frank Costello.

BANDIT: Luciano!

SLUGGER: Jesse James!

BANDIT: Billy the Kid!

BYRNE: **(Laughing.)** Fucking Genghis Khan! Ya pair o eejits. Right, listen . . .

BANDIT: Naw. Wait a minute, Johnny. Ah think we get the point. That'll be aw fine and dandy tae huv a bank account and talk aboot the businees an aw that but . . .

BYRNE: **(Annoyed and suspicious.)** But whit?

BANDIT: Well . . . do you no think you're going a wee bit far these days?

BYRNE: What are you talking about?

BANDIT: You know what ah'm talking aboot. Them two yae done over the other night wae a steakie, that's whit ahm fucking talking aboot an you know it. Wan o these days you're gonnae end up killin somebody.

BYRNE: What are you talking about? Whit's aw this aboot killin people? Huv you been drinkin?

BANDIT: You know fine well ah huvnae been drinking.

SLUGGER: An aw ah know is ah could be daein way wan right now. Cumoan tae fuck. You two wid ergue the hindlegs aff a donkey.

BYRNE: Awright. Cumoan then. You'll need tae watch that drooth o yours, Slugger. You'll be gettin a beer belly.

SLUGGER: Its better than a cut face, Johnny.

BYRNE: So's a loat o things. **(Turns back to BANDIT.)** Listen, Bandit, you must be mistaken. Ah never done over those two eejits the other night – ah don't use a steakie – did you furget that?

BANDIT: **(Resigned.)** Anything you say, Johnny.

BYRNE: Right, cumoan then, pal. Doon tae the boozers.

Percussion. They cross stage to pub area.

BYRNE: Hiya, Carole.

CAROLE: Ah've been here a whole half hoor waiting fur you.

BYRNE: That's tough kid. Whit are yae drinkin?

SLUGGER: 'Ah'm gettin thaim, Johnny.

BYRNE: That cunt Kelly wus supposed tae be here the night. Ah wunder if he's gonnae show his face.

BANDIT: He's a month overdue us it is.

BYRNE: Ah think he'll come across wae the money awright but – ta, Slugger **(SLUGGER hands in drinks.)** . . . ah think we'll need tae gie him a nice receipt fur it when he does. Just a wee reminder that yae've got tae pay up promptly.

BANDIT: A receipt. Ha, ha, That's it, We'll give him a receipt!

CAROLE: Christ, an ah thoat we wur coumin here tae relax.

SLUGGER: We are relaxing, hen.

BANDIT: Oh, oh! Here he comes!

BYRNE: Oh. There he is. The very man ah wantit tae see. Ah wis hopin we might run intae ye.

KELLY: Aye, ah knew you'd be here. Ah heard yae wur lookin fur me. Ah've goat it here. Ah'm sorry its been so long in coming. But you know how it is.

BYRNE: Naw. Ah don't know how it is, Kelly. Tell me. You were supposed tae pay back a month ago.

KELLY: Ah loast it oan the betting, Johnny. Ah just didnae huv it tae gie ye, otherwise ah'd ah gied yae it wouldn't ah?

CAROLE: Fur fuck sake wid yae listen tae that?

BYRNE: You just keep yir mouth shut. **(To KELLY.)** Right. Gie us it then.

KELLY: **(Handing over envelope.)** There you are.

BYRNE: Count it, Bandit.

BANDIT: **(A deft hand at running through the banknotes.)** Aye. Its aw here.

BYRNE: Right. Here's yir fucking receipt!

Sticks knife in KELLY's face.

Enter the windae-hingers.

LIZZIE: Hullo, Maggie. That wis an awfae cerry-oan last night, did yae see it?

MAGGIE: Naw ah wus oot ut the Bingo. Whit wis it?

LIZZIE: There wis dozens o' squad cars an' polis raided houses an' shoaps aw o'er the district and there wis blue murder.

MAGGIE: In the name o Goad whit wus goin oan?

LIZZIE: Cun yae no guess? They lift it aw that Byrne crowd in a wunner – including that whore Carole.

MAGGIE: Whit ur thae daein thaim fur?

LIZZIE: Well, that big beat polis – no that ah can stand him either – but he was telling Jack in the Dairy that thir arrestin' thaim furr everythin under the sun.

MAGGIE: Ah thoat they wir payin' the polis aff and that wis how they never went near thaim at aw.

LIZZIE: Aye. And so did everybody else. But they've done the loat o thaim.

MAGGIE: Well, hell mend thaim. That's aw ah cin say. Hell mend thaim!

Windae-hingers withdraw. Enter BANDIT, SLUGGER and BYRNE. They head for the pub.

BANDIT: **(Laughing.)** That really sickened thae bastards, didn't it?

SLUGGER: Aye. They'll no dig us up in a hurry again.

BYRNE: Ah don't know aboot that. We'll huv tae watch thaim.

BANDIT: The heid busy said he was chargin' me wae everythin under the book, but ah told him ahm sayin fuck all tae ah see ma lawyer.

SLUGGER: Aye. But ah wis worried. Ah thoat they wur gonnae dae a bit o' gardenin an start plantin some gear oan us.

BANDIT: Aye. They're better at that gemme than Percy Thrower.

BYRNE: Its just as well wee Rollo the lawyer goat there in time tae stoap them otherwise we'd be lyin in Bar by noo.

BANDIT: They really hate wee Rollo as he's the flyest mouthpiece in the business and is wide furr aw their gemms.

SLUGGER: Did yae see their faces when they hud tae let us go? It wus fuckin magic.

BYRNE: Aye but they meant business. And ah think they still mean business – especially wae me. They three I.D. Parades they gave us hid me worried. Ah thoaght they were gonnae stick some snide witnesses oanti' them tae dig us oot.

BANDIT: Aye. And imagine thaim puttin Big Kelly oan it. As if he wid dig us oot.

SLUGGER: They're fuckin idiots so they urr. Ah mean Kelly knows he deserved it. Ah cannae understand they busies.

They have entered the pub.

BANDIT: How's aboot a wee bit o service then?

BARMAN: Hullo thair, boys. Ah heard the cops dugyaes up.

BYRNE: Aye. You can say that again. Bastards! But lissen, seein' as things are a bit hoat furr us ah want yae tae keep these o'er the bar fur us

Three of them start to unload weapons.

BARMAN: Aye, sure, son. Just gie thaim tae me. Ah'll look efter thaim fur ye.

SLUGGER: **(Hauling out a meat clever.)** Noo ah don't wahnt you cuttin the heids affae pints, big yin!

BANDIT: Right noo ah've been lyin in a rotten cell aw weekend so ah want ah good bath, a burd and a right bevvy!

SLUGGER: Aye. An' we'll huv a right bevvy in here the night! **(He mimics Elvis Presley.)** Let's have a party . . . oh . . . oh . . . oh . . . let's have a party . . . ooh . . . ooh . . . ooh

BANDIT: **(Taking him up on it and dancing in front of him.)** Dancing to the Jailhouse Rock . . . Bap!

He throws out his arms and sticks out his leg on the 'bap'. At exactly the same moment two policemen appear. SLUGGER and BANDIT freeze on the spot. BYRNE is drinking with his back to them. SLUGGER makes ineffectual attempts at speech – pointing at the police and opening and closing his mouth but saying nothing. BANDIT puts a hand on BYRNE's shoulder. BYRNE looks round and takes in the policemen. He stands up slowly. Rock rhythms begin. He faces the policemen, hands loose at his side. He walks towards them. They stand on either side of him. They walk out of pub. BANDIT and SLUGGER exit after them looking furtive and trying to hide. They exit in different directions as quickly as they can.

The POLICE leave BYRNE centre stage. He is handcuffed. He is standing to attention and expressionless. If possible, the next sequence should convey by lighting and flashes that BYRNE is having his photograph taken for police files. He is taken face on. Right profile. Left profile. BANDIT and SLUGGER look in on things furtively from either side of the stage. There is no joy in their chant.

SLUGGER: Rats!

BANDIT: Rats aroon the backs!

SLUGGER: Rats aroon the backs an a wee dug!

BANDIT: It wus a rerr wee dug that.

SLUGGER: It kilt that many rats it goat a medal fur it.

BANDIT: It even goat a menshun in the paper.

Enter CAROLE.

CAROLE: Aye, boys. We're aw in it thegither. **(Sarcastic.)**

BANDIT: You shut up, ya cow. We'll keep things goin fur him while he's inside, an we'll stull be here waitin when he comes oot. Whit aboot you?

All three exit.

BYRNE: **(To audience.)** There is so much that none of you can understand about me and the world I come from and there doesn't seem to be any way of telling it that will finally get you to see the bitterness and indifference I inherited from whatever the system was the series of historical priorities that created the world into which I was born.

I didn't think. I didn't think much about it. I didn't say — there's a system — and analyse it — I was never taught to do that. But I felt. I felt strongly.

There were the haves and the have-nots. I was one of the have-nots. There were the have-nots that worked and the have-nots that thieved, then there were the rest of you — living away out there somewhere in your posh districts in aw your ease and refinement — what a situation!

It made me laugh to see you teaching your religions and holding your democratic elections — and it made me sick with disgust. That was why I enjoyed the sight of blood because, without knowing it, it was your blood I was after.

My first prison sentence was like going to university. I made a lot of new friends and useful contacts and we talked and planned together for the future. It was a top-level conference fur the world I moved in, and fur me it lasted all of two years. Maybe you'd hoped it would teach me a lesson and ah wid 'mend ma ways' so to speak. Well, it did teach me a lesson o sorts. When ah goat oot a that prison ah was ready fur somethin new — something ah had learned tae call 'crime'. Organised crime.

POLICE re-enter and march BYRNE off. Action moves to next scene — BANDIT and SLUGGER in the pub. Drinking pints.

SLUGGER: It'll no be long tae Johnny gets oot o' Bar-L noo.

BANDIT: Aye. Ah'll be glad tae see him hame again. Mind'ye he wis lucky only gettin two years fur bladin two guys.

SLUGGER: Ur you kiddin? It wis a fuckin liberty. He hud nae form.

BANDIT: Whit dyae mean? He's done his remand home, approved school and his Borstal.

SLUGGER: Aye but he's never been in Bar before.

BANDIT: Bit it wus a wee sentence fur the High Court.

SLUGGER: The last time ah saw him he wus daein his nut aboot Carole. Somebody hud telt him she wis oot at the dancin and he's no pleased aboot it.

BANDIT: Ah wunder who could ah telt him that.

SLUGGER: Ah wunder. Its no as if he's goat a loat o visitors.

BANDIT: Ach, Carole. She's a cow. She's never away fae the Barrowland an' aw that mob in the Calton urr ridin' hurr.

SLUGGER: You better no let him hear that when he gets hame.

BANDIT: Ah'm gonnae tell him. Ah'm gonnae tell him she's a midden. She deserves aw thats comin tae her.

SLUGGER: It's no Carob ah'm thinking aboot, it's Johnny. It'll break his heart.

BANDIT: That yin doesnae huv a heart. He's an animal.

CAROLE in domestic area, putting on her eye shadow. Enter BYRNE. He stands staring at her. Silent. CAROLE is using a small mirror. She sees him in it.

CAROLE: Johnny! Flings down eyeshadow brush. Naebody telt me yae were gettin oot!

BYRNE: Did thae no?

CAROLE: Oh, Johnny. It's great tae see you again.

She runs to him and puts her arms round him. BYRNE pulls them away again.

CAROLE: Whit's wrang, Johnny. Lissen, don't believe whit that Bandit says. He's just jealous. Ah've been faithful tae yae. Ah huvnae been up tae enythin . . .

BYRNE: **(Looks her up and down, taking in her clothes and her make up.)** Aye. It looks like it.

He moves towards her raising his clenched fist. He is wearing a knuckle duster.

CAROLE: Naw, Johnny. No ma face!

Enter SLUGGER and BANDIT dressed in trilbies. Long, dark-double breasted coats.

BANDIT: **(To audience.)** Mr Byrne is going places!

SLUGGER: He's in wae the Firm, the Big Boys noo. **(Arms out imitating an aeroplane.)** They fly him doon tae London. Thae meet him wae a limousine. The biggest villains in Britain.

BANDIT: And everything is very cordial. Everything is very English.

SLUGGER: Everything is layed oan — booze, gamblin, women — the loat! Nooadays oor Johnny wahnts fur nuthin!

BANDIT: An whit does he dae fur it aw in return? Just a wee bit o business.

SLUGGER: Technical business!

Enter BYRNE behind them with gun. He aims it around the audience, arm outstretched. Then smiles, twirls it in his hand and puts it in his pocket. Goes to BANDIT and SLUGGER.

SLUGGER: You know your trouble. Yae never hud enough toys tae play wae when yae wur a wean.

BYRNE: Where's the fancy-dress party then?

BANDIT: Aye, dyae like the toags. We goat them aff wee Isaac the Tailor fur a laugh tae see yae aff at the airport.

BYRNE: Ah think the man ahm gonnae meet wid like thaim. Gie's a shoat. **(Snatches hat from SLUGGERS head.)**

BYRNE is moving his head from side to side jokily with the hat on. But the other two have caught his last remark.

BANDIT: Who ur yae gonnae meet?

BYRNE: **(Straightening out, hat on his head, gun in his hand to punctuate the words.)** George Raft!

SLUGGER: Naw, cumoan. Johnny. Tell us. Who ur you gonnae meet?

BYRNE: **(Taking hat off and replacing gun in pocket.)** George Raft. Ah'm tellin yae. The Mafia.

BANDIT: Ur you serious?

BYRNE: Did yae ever know me tae tell a lie? The Mafia wahnt tae move in oan the gamblin club scene in this country an' Glasgow's wan o the target areas. They wahnt tae talk tae me because they wahnt tae keep the local boys happy wherever they go.

BANDIT: **(Suspicious.)** That's awfae big o them, is it no?

BYRNE: Its because they know if they don't cut us in they'll never get a minute's peace!

SLUGGER: Too fuckin true they widnae. Scotland fur the Scoats. Heeuch!

Bandit has detached himself from the conversation. He is looking away from the other two.

BANDIT: Aye, well that'll be aw fine an hunky-dory then wulln't it — if it aw comes aff. But the business in Glesca will huv tae go oan notwithstanding. Jist as it hud tae when you were in prison. An tonight — oan the eve o your departure fur the Big Smoke — there's wan ur two small local matters outstanding thut only Mr Byrne cun attend tae in his own inimitable style.

SLUGGER: Hear aw the big wurds?

BYRNE: What ur you tawkin about?

BANDIT: Ah'm tawkin about those two eejits up in the Cowcaddens. They've been goin aroon extortin ut the pitch an toss pools fur months – oor pitch an toss pools – an you're lettin thaim get away wae it because they've been making a name fur themself o'er where they cum fae as a coupla real hard tickets?

BANDIT looks at BYRNE challenging.

BYRNE: Ur you wahntin yir face smashed in, Bandit?

BANDIT: Aye. Yae cun smash ma face in if yae wahnt tae, Johnny, ah'm no disputin that – but it'll no get yae anywhere, Because you're slippin. You've goat that fond o yir shooter an yir fancy new pals in London thut people ur sayin yir losin yir touch. Like you say, we're aw init thegither and ah'm just thinkin aboot yir reputation because there's a helluva loat depends oan it.

BYRNE: **(Serious. Silent. Considers it all for a moment. Speaks at first as if chastened.)** Aye, well maybe there's something in what you say – **(Pause. Suddenly has BANDIT by the collar and is snarling in his face.)** But ah don't like yir way o fuckin sayin it!

Holds BANDIT by the throat for a moment then lets his hand fall and smiles, suddenly relaxed again.

BYRNE: **(Smiling.)** Right. Where ur these eejits. Take me to thaim.

Twitchy rock thing from the drums. Billy Cobham. They produce different weapons and begin to lark about, stabbing and flailing at one another. SLUGGER grabs BANDIT's head under his arm and pretends to punch it with big elaborate gestures.

SLUGGER: **(Twisting BANDIT's head about and smiling to audience.)** He wouldn't give me his lollipop so I broke his left arm! He still wouldn't give me his lollipop so I broke his right arm! And when he continued with his obstinate refusal I broke his legs, his neck, his nose, his heid, smashed in his teeth, an made his mooth tae bleed an ah goat the fuckin lollipop so there!

BYRNE is standing away from this smiling as if inspired. He has a knife in his hand. He says his words as if inspired by the knife and the general presence of violence like electricity in the air, (but not too inspired).

BYRNE: So there! So there!

BANDIT suddenly frees himself jumps up with a karate chop and howling all the way like in a Kung Fu film. From this BANDIT and SLUGGER go into a Karate routine. BYRNE starts singing vehemently.

BYRNE: When somebody loves you Its no good unless he loves you
     (Lunging with knife.) All . . . the . . . Way . . .

Suddenly they have all frozen. The drums have stopped. BYRNE has dropped his knife. They are looking over their shoulders as if being pursued and in fact we are back at the beginning of the play when we first met the Boys. They have stopped for a moment, breathless, looking back.

BANDIT: Oh my God! Oh . . . my . . . God!

BYRNE: **(Annoyed.)** Whit's the matter wae yae?

BANDIT: Whit dae yae think?

SLUGGER: Aye. Naebody sed enythin aboot fuckin murder!

Domestic interior. BYRNE and the Big Brass.

DIDI sits with her legs up on the table, flexing one to help her fix the ladder in it with a brush of nail-polish.

DIDI: Whit ah night ah've hid. Doon the Squerr. Wan efter another. Each wan mair pissed than the wan before. An it freezin. Ah hud oan this wee short skirt an ma arse wus like ice. Wan o ma regulars says tae me 'Christ Didi, yir tits ur blue!' **(Thinks.)** He's no a bad soul that yin. He aye hus a wee drink fur yae. Ah'll say that fur him. Even if it does take him hoors sometimes just tae get it up. Aw its a hard life. Ah'm another social service. Creative leisure's ma department fur aw the poor bastards thur urnae gettin it elsewhere in the natural wey o things – an ah earn every penny that ah make, you take it from me. A hard life and a dangerous wan. Ma mate Big Elsie she ust tae go aboot in Glesca the same as me wae hur big boots an hur whip under hur belt fur aw the kinky wans. But she wus a junkie – that's the kind o thing this joab makes yae dac – if yir no a junkie yir an alcoholic or yir aff yir hied ur somethin – an she ust tae dae a bit o special business doon in London frae time tae time just tae relieve the monotony, aye, well she endit up in a bedsit in Notting Hill strangled wae hur ain nylons . . .

BYRNE shouts in to her.

BYRNE: Didi! Didi!

DIDI: Who's that ut this time?

BYRNE: Its me, Johnny Byrne. Let me in quick.

DIDI: **(Opening up.)** Oh Goad, yae nivir know the minit, dae yae? **(BYRNE comes in.)** Ur yae awright?

BYRNE: Aye ahm fine. Close the door.

DIDI: What's happened?

BYRNE relaxes. Recovers composure. Smiles.

BYRNE: Nothins happened. Ah've just come roon tae see yae. Huvn't ah aye telt yae yir ma favrit Big Brass?

DIDI: Oh yae've telt me awright often enough but ah don't ever see yae unless yir in trouble. Sit doon. Wid yae like a drap o wine?

BYRNE: Aye. That wid be rerr, Didi.

DIDI: **(Extracting a bottle of Eldorado from her handbag and pouring it into cups.)** Where's Carole the night then?

BYRNE: Hingin tae mae lip!

DIDI: Aye ah widnae be surprised if she'd followed you here.

BYRNE: Ah very much doubt it.

DIDI: Johnny, whit's wrang wae yir hand? Yir bleedin. Christ, whit's been happenin, yir soaked in blood! Oh my fuck un ah huvnae a bandage nor an elastoplast in the whole place. Here, wait an ahll get a towel!

BYRNE: Its awright, Didi.

DIDI: **(She has towel)**. Its no awright at aw!

BYRNE: Its no ma blood . . . **(She withdraws from him. He smiles.)** Ah huvnae goat a mark on me.

Straight into next scene, pub interior. BYRNE rapping to SLUGGER and BANDIT.

BYRNE: OK. Right. So while ah'm away ah'm relyin oan you two tae keep things goin. There'll be a loat o money-lendin an protection tae collect ut the end o the month, and you've goat tae make sure its paid up promptly. Ah wahnt you tae cover the docks, Slugger, and Bandit, you dae aw the far away places wae strange-soundin names. Oh aye an wan o yae tell Big Wilson o'er in Partick tae screw the nut. He's still feudin wae the Anderson mob. Tell him there's supposed tae be an Amnesty. The Law ur bamboozled becos we're no aw fightin wan another eny mair.

BANDIT: We can hardly tell him that now!

BYRNE: You know sometimes you really get on my nerves, Bandit.

BANDIT: Forget it, then. Sorry ah spoke. You an yir fuckin blood lust. It makes yae say wan thing an do another. Whit aboot Grangemouth?

BYRNE: Whit aboot Grangemouth?

BANDIT: They sed thair wid be a consignment of whisky comin in if we wur interestit we could huv it cheap.

BYRNE: Cheap enough tae make it worth oor while? How many boatles?

BANDIT: Mair than enough.

BYRNE: You'd better take a van.

SLUGGER: Aye. Yae cun hire wan frae Hertz.

BANDIT: Fuck Hertz. Ah'll nick wan doon the street.

Enter CAROLE slowly. Her face is marked.

SLUGGER: Look who it is!

BYRNE and BANDIT turn and see her.

CAROLE: Johnny, can ah speak tae yae oan yir ain?

BYRNE: Ah thoat ah telt yae tae fuck off. Ah'm no wahntin tae waste ma time talkin tae you, ya whore.

CAROLE: But it's important, Johnny, It's urgent.

BYRNE: Right then. If its aw that urgent tell me it right here and now. Then get tae fuck.

CAROLE: The Law ur lookin fur yae. Tae pick yae up.

BANDIT: Och, don't give us yir worries, Carole. We've goat the Law paid aff fur miles aroon.

SLUGGER: It'll be Constable McWhirter lookin fur mair bribes.

CAROLE: It wusnae the usual polis, Johnny. They wur roon ut the hoose askin questions.

BANDIT: **(Mimics her.)** It wusnae the usual polis, Johnny.

BYRNE: **(To BANDIT.)** You shut yir mouth. **(To CAROLE.)** Whit did thae wahnt?

CAROLE: Thae wahntit tae know if ah'd been ut that party in Cowcaddens where the man was murdered.

BYRNE: Oh aye. And how did ma name get involved?

CAROLE: They thoat ah wus thair wae you.

BYRNE: An what did you say?

CAROLE: Ah sed ah hudnae seen yae and ah didnae no nothin about it.

BYRNE: Then whit did yae dae?

CAROLE: Ah came straight doon here tae warn you.

BANDIT: **(Derisive.)** Fur fucks sake. Did yae leave a trail o breadcrumbs behind yae as yae came?

CAROLE: Johnny, they said they wur gonnae get you on this wan. They're determined.

BANDIT: Ah think you'd better catch that plane, Johnny.

BYRNE: **(On his feet.)** Right. Get in touch wae Rollo the Lawyer an' tell him he might be needit.

SLUGGER: **(Exits.)** Ah'll go an get the car.

CAROLE: Johnny, you wur up in Cowcaddens that night, wurn't yae?

BYRNE: Naw. Ah wusnae near the place, wus ah, Bandit?

BANDIT: Naw!

BYRNE: They're just tryin tae hustle me because thae don't like the money-lendin.

CAROLE: Johnny, ah'm worrit aboot yae.

BANDIT: Yir a bit late in the day fur that, ur yae no?

BYRNE: You wait outside, Bandit.

BANDIT: Awright, but hurry up. Remember they might be roon here enytime.

BANDIT exits.

BYRNE takes CAROLE's face in his hand.

BYRNE: That's an awfu bad mark you've goat thair. Did somebody hit yae?

He kisses her.

BANDIT: Ur you two comin or ur yae's gonnae staun thair snoggin aw night?

BYRNE alone on stage.

BYRNE: Alright. You can look down your nose at my moneylending. But the fact was I was providing a social service. When the police finally got me they took away my address book with over three thousand addresses in it. They interviewed every person on that list but not one of them would give evidence against me. Not one of them. Because I'd been prepared to do business with them when you hadn't. While you were sitting back pretending not to notice, I had been there to care for their needs. Alright, my methods with defaulters were quick and to the point, but they weren't any different from your precious world – just a bit less hypocritical and undisguised.

Let's face it. The whole human world is a money-lending racket and if it takes a man's whole lifetime to kill him with his debts, that doesn't make it any the less an act of murder!

Explosion. SLUGGER and BANDIT run across stage behind BYRNE.

WOMAN'S VOICE: Leave us in peace! Hus there no been enough trouble already?

SLUGGER: You tell that man o yours tae keep his fuckin mouth shut or we'll be back.

Exit SLUGGER and BANDIT. Enter Clerk of Court. Police come on and handcuff BYRNE. He stands, on trial.

CLERK: **(To audience.)** My occupation is Clerk of Court. Three times I saw that man Byrne on trial for murder and twice I saw him get away with it. Witnesses disappeared. Testimony was withdrawn. Anyone who might speak against him was terrorised into silence and justice was thwarted.

On the third occasion, however, he was found Guilty: him and his cronies and his lawyer with him. It was third-time-lucky. When the Judge pronounced the sentence of life imprisonment for murder. I turned to the press benches, and the police, and even for a moment to the public gallery – and raised my thumb in triumph.

He has his thumb up and he presses it out victoriously on three sides of him.

The windows open and LIZZIE and MAGGIE appear. SLUGGER and BANDIT come on the stage, putting on prison officer's uniform.

LIZZIE: So Byrnes goat life imprisonment right enough.

MAGGIE: Aye and its good riddance tae bad rubbish. That's aw ah can say.

LIZZIE: Aye. There must huv been en evil streak in him somewhere. Its the likes o him get the Gorbals a bad name.

MAGGIE: Aye. **(Pause.)** Whit dyae think o that? The price o meat goin up agane?

LIZZIE: Oh aye. Is it no awful? Ma man says ah should make

omelettes. Ah says tae him, cun yae show me how? An he did. He made the tea last night. Omelette an chips. He said he learnt it when he wus daein his national service.

MAGGIE: Aye. It's a pity that yin, Byrne, nivir hud any national service tae dae. That wid huv knocked the nonsense oot his heid.

SLUGGER and BANDIT are now dressed in full prison officer uniform. They stand officially on either side of BYRNE. They have become the prison wardens.

BYRNE: (To audience.) I did not do the crime I was convicted for.

Drums. SLUGGER and BANDIT march off the stage with BYRNE. The CLERK OF COURT follow's behind – a little man, by the way – smiling to the audience. The Windae-hingers withdraw.

The Sweetest of Songs is the Song of the Clyde.

Act 2

BYRNE on bunk. Prison cell. MOCHAN in next cell listening. BYRNE direct to audience.

BYRNE: When a man goes into prison, he's suddenly cut off. His old friends disappear, and his wife, his family – how can he possibly keep in touch wae them when he's locked away.

He hears that his son's getting into trouble, following in his father's footsteps, but he can do nothing about it. The walls prevent him. The thick walls of justice. Your justice.

Enter JOHNSTONE, Prison Officer. Furtive.

JOHNSTONE: Byrne! Byrne! You're a faither. Your burds just hud a baby.

BYRNE: When?

JOHNSTONE: Last night. Its a girl.

BYRNE: A girl? Ur they awright?

JOHNSTONE: Aye, they're fine. There's somebody coming. I'll need to go. **(Exits.)**

BYRNE: Naw. Don't go. Come back. Listen! Listen! **(To audience.)** So yir daein time. That's a good phrase for it. Daein time. Because that's whit yir daein awright. Time! Time with no distractions. Plenty of time tae consider the matter. Time tae burn. Time tae waste. Time tae kill.

One year. Two year. Three year. Four.

And if yir lucky you've goat a window you can see through, and if you're even luckier through that window you can see a tree, and you think about the day when you'll see the other side of that tree.

Beans. Sweat. Urine. Insomnia.

Tries to catch a fly.

Poor me. Poor fly. Sharing a cell.

Five year. Six year. Seven year. More.

Thick. Thick. Walls of justice.

Thick. Thick. Heads of justice.

Thick. Thick. Assholes of justice.

Thick. Thick. Whores of justice.

— who do you think you are locking me up in here and telling me it's for life? Telling me I deserve it? My life. Fullstop. Thank you very much. I'm so grateful to you for giving me what I deserve. It must be nice to be in the right because it's shitty to be in the wrong

JOHNSTONE: Your lawyer's here for you, Byrne.

BYRNE turns as LEWIS, lawyer, enters.

LEWIS: Sorry I couldnae get here sooner, Johnny. How are you?

BYRNE: In a wee bit o a hurry tae get oot o here.

LEWIS: They've put you in solitary.

BYRNE: Aye well there's a fly up in the corner up there. He an me huv been huving a wee bit o a blether. How's Carole?

LEWIS: She's fine, Johnny. She's at home with her mother.

BYRNE: That old bag. Tell hur no tae be giein the wean any o her cheap biddy.

LEWIS: Does she drink?

BYRNE: The old woman? Christ, she'd drink the Clyde dry if it wis full o whisky.

LEWIS: You don't need to worry about the baby. Carole will look after her alright. You can trust her.

BYRNE: Trust her nothing. Lewis, ah wahnt out o here and fast. Ah lay doon oan ma bunk last night an a thoat, fifteen years. Fifteen fuckin years. That old swine ae a judge an' the police lieing their mooths aff. How long wull it take fur the Appeal tae come through?

LEWIS: Johnny, I wouldnae pin any hopes on an appeal. They were out tae get you. One way or another. The walls of that court would have had to fall down before you'd have walked out of there a free man. **(BYRNE is silent.)** I don't suppose you'll have seen your press.

Hands BYRNE newspapers.

BYRNE: **(Reading.)** 'I was a victim of The Gentle Terror!' Whit's aw this about?

LEWIS: Did you no know? That's the name you go under in the Glasgow underworld. Read further down.

BYRNE: 'Father of four William Brown told of the night he was threatened by . . . John Byrne, better known, as The Gentle Terror, who said that if he didn't pay his debt, he would cut off his ears!' Jesus Christ! These people have got wonderful imaginations!

LEWIS: You're good copy, Johnny. There's no a good word to say about yae.

BYRNE: And will that affect the appeal?

LEWIS: Well, it shoudnae but it gives you an indication. They're gloating, Johnny. And now they've got you, they're no gonnae let you go without a struggle. The best you can hope for is a bit of remission and parole from time to time – if you keep your nose clean. And your hands to yourself. I know it won't be easy but I would be misleading you if I told you otherwise.

BYRNE silent, thinking.

BYRNE: Why did they put me in solitary, Lewis?

LEWIS: Because of your reputation, Johnny. You're a dangerous man.

Pause. BYRNE thinks again before he speaks.

BYRNE: Aye. Well, ah'm no gonnae stop being dangerous, just because ah'm in here. If thae think ahm gonnae crawl fur a bit o parole, they've goat another think comin.

LEWIS: A few years ago they would have hanged you.

BYRNE: They're gonnae wish they hud.

Enter MOCHAN, sweeping the stage.

MOCHAN: Hello there. Ma name's Michael Mochan. Ah've goat a story too. But youse'll no be wantin tae be bothert wae that. Ah mean, ah'm just an old lag, who wahnts tae know whit ah think? Ah dae keep ma nose clean **(Wipes it.)** so ah get wee joabs tae dae an ah get aboot mair than the rest o thaim. An that way ah get tae hear a loat an' see a loat, an usually ah keep my mooth shut aboot it, but wae the things that happened tae that man, Byrne, well, the time came when ah knew ah couldnae just sit back and watch any loanger, ah wis gonnae huv tae say whit ah hud seen, whatever it cost me . . . No that it made much difference.

(Pause. Thinks.) Ach, but that aw comes later when ah goat tae know him. So ah'll talk tae yaes later oan − if that's awright. Ah jist thoat ah'd say hello an introduce masel.

Exits.

Enter BYRNE, CAROLE and JOHNSTONE.

BYRNE: Whereas the wean?

CAROLE: Ah left hur wae ma muther.

BYRNE: Yae whit? Ur ye aff yir heid?

CAROLE: Ah knew yae'd wahnt tae see hur but ah wus feart she catch the cauld.

BYRNE is exasperated. He looks at JOHNSTONE who is standing by.

BYRNE: Can you no wait ootside fur a while?

JOHNSTONE: Sorry Johnny. Ah've goat ma orders.

BYRNT: Aye, awright. Yir no a bad cunt, Johnstone. Ah wish there were mair like you in this shithoose. **(To CAROLE.)** It wus him telt me aboot the wean. Otherwise ah'd never huv known. That's the way they treat you in this fuckin place. Huv yae seen Danny?

CAROLE: He's lying low.

BYRNE: Ah'll bet he is, the old bastard. The rest o us inside an' he goes Scotfree. Typical. Ah'll bet he's drinking himsel paralytic. Old swine.

CAROLE: Thae wur aw tawkin aboot you in the hoaspital.

BYRNE: Wur they?

CAROLE: Aye. Aw the women. Lying thair feeding thair weans an you wur the main topic o conversation. You should ah heard the things thae wur sayin.

BYRNE: Ah've seen the papers.

CAROLE: It wus worse than the papers. Wan wife sed yae impaled somebody on the spike o a railin, another wan said yae tortured a man by nailing his feet tae the floor. An thir wus this big fat bitch thair, it was hur eigth, and she sed you wur a hired gun doon in London.

BYRNE: An whit did you say?

CAROLE: Ah never said anythin. Ah kept ma mooth shut.

BYRNE: Ur yae ashamed o me then?

CAROLE: Well, whit dae yae expect me tae dae, haud the wean up an tell them you loat just watch whit yir sayin Byrne's this wean's father.

BYRNE: Well you might've stoaped them tellin lies aboot me at least.

CAROLE: How dae ah know if its lies. Ah don't know how many people you've kilt, dae ah?

BYRNE: Well ah'll tell yae. Ah've never kilt anybody in ma fuckin life – and don't you furget it. **(CAROLE Looking away. Then to JOHNSTONE.)** – Can ah gie him a cigarette? **(JOHNSTONE nods assent.)** She produces cigarettes from her bra.

BYRNE: Whit ur yae daein?

CAROLE: Thae take everythin aff yae doon thair. **(Lights cigarette for him. One for herself.)** That yin Halliday's cerryin oan like a big shoat noo that you're inside.

BYRNE: Whit's he daein?

CAROLE: He wus in the pub last night an he smashed the gantry.

BYRNE: Eeejit!

CAROLE: Tommy the barman says thair aw fighting like cats an doags because you're no thair tae keep the peace.

BYRNE: Aye well you tell Tommy ah'll see tae thaim soon enough.

CAROLE: How come?

BYRNE: Because ah'm getting out o here, that's how come.

CAROLE: Naebday telt me aboot it. When ur yae getting out?

BYRNE: Ah'll no bother, if that's how you feel aboot it. Ah'll just stay here.

CAROLE: Och don't talk stupit!

BYRNE: Whit's the matter wae you? Huv yae goat yirsel a new man awready?

CAROLE: Look ah huvnae goat time tae took fur fellas, ah'm too busy lookin efter your fuckin wean.

BYRNE raises his arm. JOHNSTONE moves to restrain him.

BYRNE: Aw, don't worry, Johnstone, old boy. She's no worth it. Ur yae married yirself?

JOHNSTONE: Aye.

BYRNE: Any family?

JOHNSTONE: A boy and a girl.

BYRNE: Good fur you!

CAROLE: Wull you stoap talking tae that swine an tell me whit this is aw aboot?

BYRNE: Whit? Oh, ur you still here? Awright, ah'll tell yae. Now listen carefully fur wance in yir life. This is important. Its aboot ma Appeal.

CAROLE: Oh, is that aw.

BYRNE: Whit dae yae mean 'is that aw'?

CAROLE: Well, Lewis hus telt me aw aboot it.

BYRNE: Lewis doesnae huv enything tae dae wae it anymore.

CAROLE: Huv yae changed yir lawyer?

BYRNE: Aye.

CAROLE: Who huv yae goat? Franchetti?

BYRNE: That balloon. You must be jokin.

CAROLE: Who then?

BYRNE: Maself.

CAROLE: You? Since when did you become a lawyer?

BYRNE: **(Sits back and regards her with disgust.)** Look ut yae, ya stupit wee whore. Of course ah'm no a lawyer, fur fuck sake, Ah'm no pretendin tae be a lawyer, but can you no understand anything? Do you no understand anything at all? No even aboot me?

This is ma life ah'm fighting fur. You've hud a wean tae me an ah wahnt tae see it. No in here. Ah'm glad you didnae bring it in here. Because ah don't wahnt it tae see its faither in a place like this

CAROLE: It happens to be a she.

BYRNE: Ah thoat a telt you tae listen.

CAROLE: Awright, ah'm listening.

BYRNE: OK. This is ma life ah'm fightin fur and nobody can fight fur ma life except me maself. But ah'm gonnae need new witnesses and ah wahnt you tae talk tae a few people fur me. Do you understand that?

CAROLE: Which people?

BYRNE: **(Hesitates. Speaks to JOHNSTONE.)** Could you stoap up yir ears fur a minit. Johnstone?

JOHNSTONE: Ah'm afraid the time's up. Johnny.

BYRNE: Aye but we've goat drinkin up time. **(Returns to CAROLE.)** Go doon tae the pub and talk tae the Big Yin.

CAROLE: Wullie?

BYRNE: Aye! An' tell him tae talk tae that mob in Shamrock Street an tell thaim ah'll be wahntin tae see thaim up here.

CAROLE: Who do you mean in Shamrock Street?

BYRNE: Never mind that. Just tell him. He'll know whit ahm talking aboot.

JOHNSTONE: Awright, that's the time.

CAROLE: **(Annoyed at JOHNSTONE.)** Och, awright. Ah'm just goin.

BYRNE: Come here. **(She goes to him.)** Dae's a favour Johnstone an close yir eyes a wee minit. **(They kiss.)** Noo don't you furget that. And next time bring the wean in so that ah can see it.

Enter MOCHAN.

MOCHAN: The course of young love never runs smooth. Aye, well he's making a big mistake handling that Appeal himsel. They'll no like that. There was only one man ah ever knew that managed to really speak the truth in a Court of Law and that wus an old wino ah knew. A right old down-and-outer, reeling aboot in the streets wae a three-week stubble oan his chin an stoapin people fur the price of a cup o tea. An niver even goat tae know his name. But ah saw his grand finale in the Sheriff Court in Glasgow wan day, when he goat tae his feet swayed fae side tae side straightened himsel up took a deep breath an made a speech oan his own behalf. This wus him:

Today ah wish tae apologise. Ah wish tae apologise tae ma wife fur the terrible life ah gied hur tae ma children – who no longer want to speak to me – fur aw they hud tae go without because of their father – tae aw the people – doctors and police social workers and ministers of religion – who tried tae give me help only tae huv the help thrown back in their face and most of all – most of all, he said, and he swayed a wee bit – most of all ah want tae apologise tae this Court in its Mercy fur the many times ah spurned its Clemency. Ah apologise!

The whole Court was stunned intae silence. And the Sheriff leaned forward and said, 'Is there anything you would like to add?' And the old fella looked up and he smiled and he opened out his arms and he closed his eyes tilted back his head, and this is whit he said: **(Sings.)**

I left my heart
In San Francisco . . .

BYRNE: Your Worship, Ladies and Gentlemen of the Jury, and all the rest of you wankers out there, here ah ahm, the animal, wae a great big lawbook in ma hand an thinking.

The animal is thinking. He's beginning tae figure it out. Whit yir legal racket's aw about, he's sussed it.

So ah thoat ah wus a fly-boy. Ah thoat ah wus hard. But you loat take the biscuit. Yae beat the band. You've goat the biggest racket of aw and you're the coolest customers because you're legal – and ahm no?

Ah huvnae done any more than the rest o you ur daein every livin day o your free lifes, you're just a bit mair lang-distance aboot it, yae've goat a wee bit finesse – but everything you've goat depends oan thievin and killin o one kind or another – the only difference is that you make the Laws!

But remember this, the animal is thinking.

MOCHAN has been standing, leaning on his brush and watching BYRNE throughout the speech.

MOCHAN: Oh, my Goad, son, yir like a wild stallion wae a man oan its back. Why don't yae just give up an' gie yirsel peace? Yir an awfae hard man.

(To audience.) But he was never hard enough because he couldnae keep control o himself. He suffered frae frustration. He hud aw this energy bilin up inside him an he couldnae get it oot.

So there would always come a moment when he wid snap an it wid come oot o him like a torrent. An that wus his undoin. Fur aw that he wus thinkin, he felt too much, an' he let his feelins run away wae him.

It wus because o that he never actually goat tae make his appeal as you'll see in a minit. The famous story ah'm sure you've never heard aboot – 'Johnny Byrne Meets the Commando' better unknown as brawn beats its brains oot agen –

Exits with brush.

Attention returns to BYRNE.

Enter Second Prison Officer, RENFREW, closely followed by the COMMANDO who is Assistant Governor of the prison.

RENFREW: OK, Byrne. Oan yir feet. The Assistant Governor's here tae see yae.

BYRNE: The Assistant Governor. What's he wanting?

RENFREW: Don't be impudent. Get on your feet.

BYRNE: Just a minute. Who do you think you're talking to?

COMMANDO: OK, Renfrew, outside. I'll deal with this alone.

RENFREW: Are you sure, sir?

RENFREW: I'll be right outside, sir.

BYRNE: Yes, sir. No, sir. Three bags full, sir.

COMMANDO: You wanted to see me, Byrne.

BYRNE: Ah don't, what gives you that impression. I could think o nicer sights.

COMMANDO: Don't smart-talk me, Byrne. You've been demanding to see someone for the last ten days.

BYRNE: Aye, that's right. Ah think it wis ten days. Might huv been eleven. Ah'm no sure. You lose track of time in this place. You know whit ah mean? Aye but ah think you're right, now that you come to mention it ah huv been asking tae see someone, but ah widnae huv said ah wus **(demanding.)** anything, and ah don't think the person ah wus asking tae see is you. Ah wanted tae see the guvnor, no his assistant. And by the way, ah'll smart-talk you anytime ah like.

COMMANDO: How dare you, Byrne. I won't have talk like this in my prison.

BYRNE: Oh, it's your prison, is it? Ah wus beginnin tae wunder who owned it. Ah knew it certainly didnae belang tae me. Ah wid huv arranged the furniture different.

COMMANDO: You can make things worse for yourself, you know.

BYRNE: No much worse, surely.

COMMANDO: Yes, but you can make things easy for yourself or you can make them hard, depending on how you behave.

BYRNE: Ha! Ha! That's funny. That's . . . that's 'rich', as they say, me behave maself ah'm no capable of behavin maself can you people no understand that? Oh, you're a joke so yae ur, comin intae me daein a lifer and telling me tae behave maself. You behave yourself. Awright, so if you've been sent doon tae talk tae the animal yae might as well talk tae the animal. The animal is hoping you have to discuss the witnesses fur its Appeal.

COMMANDO: No, I haven't come here to discuss. I've come here to tell you something. There's nothing to discuss.

BYRNE: Oh? And what is there to tell me?

COMMANDO: You're not going to be allowed to interview the witnesses. Not in this prison. If you want to have witnesses interviewed, you'll have to get a Lawyer to do it for you.

BYRNE: But I'm handling my Appeal myself. I'm entitled to interview witnesses to prepare my case.

COMMANDO: Not if I think there might be a security risk involved.

BYRNE: What?

COMMANDO: I think you heard what I said.

BYRNE: Aye. Ah heard you awright. Ah just couldnae believe what ah wus hearing. Ah don't think you know this, china, but ah know you. You're the wan thae call the Commando. That's the wurd you like tae put aboot this place — that yir wan o the real dirty squad that fought against old Adolf. The Commando. Aye, yir reputations preceded yae.

COMMANDO: And I've dealt with harder men than you, Byrne.

BYRNE: Maybe you have. Maybe yae huvnae.

COMMANDO: But thae never had so much to say for themselves as you seem to have.

BYRNE: You'll have to excuse me. You know, it must've been that life imprisonment sentence the judge passed oan me, it must have give me a shock or something but a strange thing has happened since ah came in here — ah've started thinking. And now that ah've started, ah just cannae seem tae stop. And wan o the things ah've been thinking, it's a funny thing this but I don't really think you think there's a security risk involved at all, you don't seriously think ah wid try tae escape, dae yae? Naw. You're just withholding ma witnesses frae me because Grabs hold of him you're so . . . fucking . . . vindictive!

COMMANDO: You let go of me, Byrne.

BYRNE: Naw. Ah'm no letting go o you until you tell me ah'm getting your signature on that piece of paper that ah need!

He is holding THE COMMANDO with one hand and forming up the other into a clenched fist under his face. THE COMMANDO speaks nervously over his shoulder.

COMMANDO: Renfrew?

BYRNE finally loses patience and smashes him in the face, snarling with disgust.

COMMANDO: Officer! Officer! Come quickly!

BYRE has let go of him and is laughing happily at the sight of THE COMMANDO lying on the floor. RENFREW and JOHNSTONE run in. They grab BYRNE from behind, one on either arm, BYRNE is still laughing happily. THE COMMANDO gets up and straightens himself out.

COMMANDO: You'll hear more of this, Byrne.

BYRNE is still laughing. This next bit is fast. He breaks in mid-laugh and suddenly he is serious, concentrated. Then he swings up, using the grip of the screws as a lever, taking both feet off the ground and kicking him hard in the groin. THE COMMANDO keels over. Grunting with the pain. RENFREW leaves go of his grip on BYRNE and goes to COMMANDO's assistance. BYRNE has relaxed. JOHNSTONE keeps a grip on his arm but perhaps it is not so intense as it was a moment before. As RENFREW speaks to JOHNSTONE, he is bundling THE COMMANDO out of the Cell.

RENFREW: Ah think you'd better lock him up. Ah seem tae remember he's a pal o yours.

JOHNSTONE locks cell door. BYRNE shouts through it, laughing, his hands up at his mouth – cupped.

BYRNE: (**Shouting.**) *Some fuckin commando*!

His laughter dies away and he is sobbing and gasping. He is desperate and sad. He escapes down the door with his hands, the side of his face pressed against it. He lies on the floor silent, his face resting forehead-down on his arm.

Percussion.

MOCHAN: That wus just before ah met up wae him. That wus the beginning o the end wae Byrne and prison. Or maybe you should say the beginning of the ending because it husnae ended yet. Anyway, a strange thing happened in a Glasgow Court following the events just seen. The charge was read out that the accused, John Byrne, had, on such-and-such a day, assaulted a senior prison officer, That wus awright. Nothin unexpected aboot that. Whit wis strange wus the next bit. His lawyer gets up and says:

LEWIS has walked on during these last words. He delivers his speech formally out to the audience. Immediately after making his speech he exits. No personal contact is made with audience.

In behind MOCHAN and LEWIS' speeches, BYRNE is set upon by RENFREW and JOHNSTONE who force him, struggling, into a straight-jacket. Both men are hitting him with batons. Eventually they have him in strait-jacket. RENFREW continues hitting him long after might be considered necessary. JOHNSTONE restrains him. BYRNE is left lying on the stage. The strait-jacket is saturated in blood.

LEWIS: I am unable to defend my client on this charge because I have not been able to find him. When I went to the prison to prepare his defence, I was told he had been taken away but no-one would tell me where . . .

Exit LEWIS.

MOCHAN: Ah knew where he wus and ah saw the state he came in. He wus in Peterheid and he wus in the solitary block where ah used tae dae some o ma sweeping. And that wus where the real troubles started. Because, among other things, that's where he

71

met a big screw called Paisley. Ah'll tell yae mair aboot him later an ye'll see a wee bit fur yirsel.

BYRNE is on stage in strait-jacket. He struggles to get out of it. At first there is percussion. Then there is only his voice as a stab against the silence.

BYRNE: Fuck! Fuck, Fuck! Fuck You!

Fuck You, You Bastards.

Fuck You Fuck You Fuck You.

The percussion answers the rhythm. Builds to a crescendo when he bursts the strait-jacket. Then he is on his knees facing the audience. He opens out his arms and roars. He falls slowly backwards, arching himself in a yoga asana. The back of his head (nape of neck) and his heels (soles) touch the floor, but his back is arched between them. What do his arms do? Please see, I. S. Iyengar's 'Light on Yoga' for further details. Gradually this can be relaxed. MOCHAN approaches and looks in at him. BYRNE is flat on his back.

MOCHAN: Johnny Byrne!

BYRNE: Who's there?

MOCHAN: It's Michael Mochan.

BYRNE: Hello there, Michael. Nice tae meet yae. Ah've heard a loat aboot yae. How ur yae daein old-timer?

MOCHAN: Ah'm daein fine. An' what aboot yirsel? An' less o the old-timer.

BYRNE: Ah'm awright. At least ah'm here. Ah've arrived. But it wus a rough journey getting here. Ah think ah'm suffering fae screw-lag. Wid yae mind just telling me where ah ahm?

MOCHAN: Christ, dae yae no even know that? Did they no even tell

ye where they were taking yae? You're in Peterheid. Solitary
detention wing. Yir no allowed any visitors ur nuthin, so ye'll huv
tae make the best o me. Ah'm the only conversation yir gonnae
get in here that is nae a crack in the heid. Ah hear yae burst yir
straight-jacket.

BYRNE: Ach, it wus weakened. It wus ma ain blood that weakened
it. It wus saturated.

MOCHAN: They must huv gied yae some goins over. Wus that done
before yae goat here or wus some o it done after?

BYRNE: Some ae it wus here. There's a big bastard aroon here an
he wus knockin fuck oot o me. Ah hud tae crack him oan the jaw.

MOCHAN: Did he huv a moustache?

BYRNE: He might huv hud. Ah wusnae really hoping ah'd ever huv
tae identify the bastard agen. Aye, but a think he did.

MOCHAN: That sounds like him.

BYRNE: Who in particular?

MOCHAN: Paisley. Some o us caw him the Reverend because he
hates aw Catholics. Wae a name like yours, your a gonner. He's
a sadistic big bastard. And there's been several cases of
brutalisation in this prison because o him in the last two months.

BYRNE: Aye. Well ah'm gonnae get tae the governor aboot him.

MOCLIAN: He's been had up two or three times but he always gets
away wae it. The last time it was fur buggering two of the young
prisoners. Everybody knew he'd done it, including his own
lawyer, and when he got him off wae it, he wus sick. The lawyer
was sick. So there you are, even his own lawyer.

BYRNE: Aye, well let him come for me. I'll be ready for him.

MOCHAN: Did you say you'd cracked his jaw?

BYRNE: That's right.

MOCHAN: Well, don't you worry. He'll be coming for you alright.

Drums. A march. Enter PAISLEY, JOHNSTONE and RENFREW. They face straight on to the audience. PAISLEY is one step in front of the other two who form the tips of a triangle behind him. He speaks direct to the audience.

PAISLEY: I'm Paisley. I'm the one. The bad screw. The one who brings disrepute on all his hard-working colleagues who are making the best of a very tough job. I'm the sadist. The one that's got too much of a taste for the sight of blood. That's what they say. I know it only too well. The prisoners don't like me because they know I don't mess about. I believe in discipline and I believe in using hard methods to tame hard men. And the other **(Pause.)** screws don't like me because they know I'm the one that does the dirty work for them.

They know what this prison would be like if we didn't get tough from time to time. They don't want to walk in fear of their life from day to day when they're going about their job, any more than you would. So they tolerate me. I'm **(their)** hard man. And they feel a wee bit guilty about me because I'm an aspect of themselves they don't like to admit to. Just like you should be feeling guilty about us because we're the garbage disposal squad for the social sewage system. You people out there, that's the way it works for you — you've got a crime problem so you just flush it away one thug after another in behind bars and safely locked away. The cistern's clanked and you can think you can leave it floating away from you to the depths of the sea. Well, ah've goat news fur you — its pollution. Yir gonnae huv tae look ut it. Because if yae don't, wun day its gonnae destroy yae. But in the meantime, dirties like me, well, lets just say we're a necessary evil. Very necessary.

BYRNE and MOCHAN: **(Together)** Screws! Screws!

On the chant of 'Screws Screws' the drums start their march

again. **The Three SCREWS march over to BYRNE's cell. Drums stop when they are ranged around BYRNE. Important that MOCHAN observes all that is happening.**

PAISLEY: OK, Byrne. On your feet. You're going for a wee walk.

BYRNE: Where are you taking me?

PAISLEY: For a wash. You stink.

BYRNE: It doesnae take three of you to take me for a wash.

JOHNSTONE: Come on, Johnny, it's OK.

BYRNE: Johnstone! Ur you followin me or somethin?

RENFREW: Come on. Get these on. **(Puts on handcuffs.)** We'll decide on staffing in this prison, no you.

BYRNE: **(To Paisley.)** Could ah no be handcuffed tae somebody else? This guy's breath stinks. Ah'm sure you'd be much nicer.

PAISLEY: Cumon, Byrne, get going and keep the mouth shut. You're going to have plenty of chance tae talk. We've goat one or two questions to ask you.

BYRNE: Wait a minute. What's all this about? I might've known you lot wouldnae give a fuck supposin ah never washed fae wan year tae the next.

PAISLEY: **(Pushing him.)** Cumon, get moving.

BYRNE: Watch it! Paisley. On second thoughts, you stink more than he does.

PAISLEY threatens him.

BYRNE: That's right, ya coward. Ah know all about you. You used tae be a hitman fur the moneylender doon the docks. Did yir 'colleagues' know that?

PAISLEY hits him. BYRNE spits at PAISLEY. PAISLEY enraged. JOHNSTONE restrains him.

JOHNSTONE: Take it easy.

PAISLEY: Cumon, move him.

Drums. They move Byrne out of cell towards a sink which represents the washroom. As they cross stage to it, BYRNE is tugging and pulling at the handcuff which attaches him to RENFREW. The effect should be comic. MOCHAN follows them across and watches from a concealed position.

PAISLEY: OK, Byrne. Get in there.

BYRNE Ah'm no going in there. No wae the three o you and no
    witnesses.

MOCHAN makes a thumbs-up sign to the audience to let them know he is keeping an eye on things.

PAISLEY: **(Pushing him roughly.)** Get in!

RENFREW: **(Who has been pulled off balance by PAISLEY's pushing.)** Hey, go easy!

BYRNE: **(Now in wash area.)** Aye, you heard whit the man said.

PAISLEY: OK. Byrne. We're taking the handcuffs off, but no funny
    business. There's a sinkful of water for you tae wash yourself.

The handcuffs are removed. BYRNE looks at them all as if he might start some trouble but then he turns away laughing scornfully, as if he has decided they are not worth the effort. He sits down at the sink and enjoys the water.

BYRNE: Oh, this is rerr. Ah suppose you thoat animals like me
    wouldnae like water. Did yae bring the DDT powder too?

PAISLEY: Give him the towel.

JOHNSTONE gives him a towel which BYRNE takes reluctantly.

BYRNE Is that aw the wash ah'm gonnae get? Fur fuck's sake, ah never even goat time tae dae behind ma ears. Whit aboot a shave. Surely youse can run as far as a shave. Or is shaving forbidden too?

PAISLEY: You're damn right its forbidden. We know what you do wae a razor, Byrne. Dry yourself off. Ah've goat some questions tae ask yae.

BYRNE: Oh ho! This is when we find out what its all about, eh? **(Dries his face.)** OK, fire away. Paisley. I'm intrigued. **(Aside to RENFREW, quickly.)** You didnae think ah'd know a word like that, did yae, Renfrew?

PAISLEY: Stoap playing the innocent, Byrne. What's aw this aboot a prisoner's charter?

BYRNE: What? A prisoner's charter. Don't ask me, Ian, ah don't know anything aboot anything as intelligent as that. Ah'm an animal.

PAISLEY: We've found a copy of it in the main block and we know you're behind it. There's been nothing but trouble since you were brought here.

BYRNE: What does it say?

PAISLEY: You know fucking well what it says. A more humane system and investigations . . . investigations of brutality in this prison . . .

BYRNE: That sounds like interesting reading. Ah wouldnae mind a copy o that if yae can spare wan.

PAISLEY: **(Threatening.)** Don't mess with me, Byrne. What's going oan? You'd better tell us or its more than your life's worth.

BYRNE: **(Thinks about it.)** Ah'm tellin you nothing.

PAISLEY: Awright! Give him a duckin.

They force BYRNE's head under water. He struggles throughout.

JOHNSTONE: Will we bring him up?

PAISLEY: Naw. Keep him down a minute longer. We'll make him talk. Don't you worry.

JOHNSTONE: We'd better be careful.

PAISLEY: Listen, son. Don't you try tae tell me. How long huv you been in the prison service?

JOHNSTONE: Two years.

PAISLEY: Aye, well ah'm comin up fur ten years. So you just keep yir mouth shut. **(Pause)** OK. Let him up . . .

BYRNE is released from the water. He shakes his head about and starts shouting as he does so, struggling with RENFREW and JOHNSTONE.

BYRNE: Fuck you, you homosexual bastard, Paisley, and fuck King Billy!

PAISLEY: OK. Give him another ducking. **(They hesitate.)** Go on, do it. **(They do.)** Fur fuck sake, do you see whit he's like. Kindness'll get you nowhere wae that yin. OK. Bring him up again.

BYRNE: Fuck!

PAISLEY: Awright, Byrne. You'd better start talking or you'll go under a third time and this time you won't come back up.

BYRNE looks up at him slowly, thinking things over.

BYRNE: Awright. So what is it you want to know?

PAISLEY: There's something being planned. Some kind of unrest among the men.

BYRNE: That's right.

PAISLEY: What is it?

BYRNE: They're gonnae cut your balls off. **(PAISLEY hits him.)** They're gonnae cut your balls off an' then they're gonnae serve thaim up tae the governor oan toast.

PAISLEY: OK. Put him under again. And this time . . . **(they have his head under water.)** This time . . . don't bother . . . tae bring him up!

In darkness, noise of prison riot begins. Men's voices shouting. Various sounds emerge clearly from it. 'Up on the Roof'. Perhaps the Prisoner's Charter is read out at this point. Last sound to emerge across the crowd noise is a voice through a public address hailer:

'If you come down peacefully, with no trouble, there will be no recriminations . . . I repeat that . . . no recriminations if you come down peacefully . . .'

BYRNE is lying on his bunk. MOCHAN speaks through to him excitedly.

MOCHAN: Johnny, waken up. Quick. There's a riot. The men ur up oan the roof an the press and television's here an everything . . .

BYRNE: **(Groggy.)** What?

MOCHAN: They're demanding an investigation into prison brutality . . . Oh, ur you awright. Christ, ah thoat they wur gonnae go the whole way wae yae that time. Johnny. If Paisley hud hud his way, they wid have, but Johnstone chickened oot o it.

BYRNE: Ah must ah blacked out.

MOCHAN: You're lucky yir lungs didnae burst.

Sound of loudhailer in distance.

BYRNE: What's that?

MOCHAN: They're bringing them down. They've been telt that if they come doon peacefully there'll be no recriminations against the ringleaders.

BYRNE: Thank Christ fur that. They think ah'm the masterplanner. Masturbator's more fucking like it. Shower o wankers!

MOCHAN: Sssh! Listen!

Man howling in the distance.

MOCHAN: It sounds as if they're bringing thaim up here to the solitary wing.

BYRNE: Aye, and that doesnae sound much like 'no recriminations'. **(Man's voice shouting louder.)** 'They're kicking me, boys. Leave me alane. Ah hud nothin tae dae wae it'.

BYRNE: So much fur reason. So much fur the peaceful approach. Bastards!

MOCHAN and BYRNE: **(Together). (Banging and making as much noise as possible.)** Bastards! Bastards! Bastards! Bastards!

Percussion. The March again. Screws enter to BYRNE. BYRNE immediately on the ready for a fight.

PAISLEY: You've been creating a bit of a din doon here, Byrne. Did yae think we wouldnae hear you?

BYRNE: Ah wahntit yae tae hear me because ah could hear whit you were up tae ya dirty swine. You're a pig. A disgusting Protestant pig.

RENFREW: Look at him, the animal, ready fur anuther fight.

BYRNE: That's right, crabcrutch, ah'm ready fur you enytime.

They pull their batons.

BYRNE: Oh, its the big sticks, is it? Gie me wan and ah'll ram it up yir arse.

JOHNSTONE: Don't make things worse fur yourself, Johnny.

BYRNE: Aw, cumon, less o the old pals act wae that thing in yir haun. Whit's the matter wae you loat enyway? Wull your old ladies no let yae get it in anymore? Is this how yae ease yir frustrations?

PAISLEY: **(To others.)** Haud him. **(They grab hold of BYRNE PAISLEY speaks to him with the baton held back, viciously ready for action.)** I'm going to enjoy this, Byrne. Aye, you're right. It is frustration. There's been a loat o faces ah've wahntit tae punch and couldnae an' a loat of skulls ah've wahntit tae crack — and couldnae. But wae you ah've got a perfect excuse tae let it aw come out . . .

BYRNE kicks him and at the same time jumps on RENFREW. He jabs his fingers repeatedly in RENFREW's eye, finally getting a hold on the eye, straining as if to gouge it out. He is pulled off by JOHNSTONE and PAISLEY beats him about the head with his baton. RENFREW lies howling on the floor, his hand over his injured eye.

RENFREW: Ma eye! Ma eye! What's he done tae ma eye!

PAISLEY: Aw shut up. You'll survive. **(Kicks BYRNE who is unconscious.)** And so will he. Worst luck. Ah think he'll need tae go tae a special place. A very special place.

JOHNSTONE: **(He is helping RENFREW.)** Listen, Paisley, there's bound to be an inquiry about this. Renfrew's injured.

PAISLEY: Yes. You're quite right, Johnstone. There probably will be an inquiry. But that's no gonnae bother us, is it? No unless you start getting loose wae yir tongue.

JOHNSTONE: But they'll see the marks on his head.

PAISLEY: That's because he fell on the floor, whilst attacking a prison officer, isn't it? You saw it with your own eyes. You did see it, didn't you?

JOHNSTONE: . . . Fell on the floor . . . They'll never accept that.

PAISLEY: They've accepted it before. Plenty o times. Come on. We'd better get this yin tae a doctor. **(To audience)**. Listen, if you excuse him **(indicates)** BYRNE on the grounds that he's a product of this shit-heap system, then you'd better excuse me on the same grounds.

Drums. They exit.

BYRNE stands up slowly, composes himself, and walks out of cell towards audience. Before he speaks he smiles. He begins his speech by mimicking the upperclass tones of a Judge.

BYRNE: Ladies and Gentlemen of the Jury. In this trial, as in all criminal trials, the Judge and the Jury have different tasks. Your task is, at the end of the day, to bring in a verdict on the Charge on the Indictment before you. **(Own voice.)** The trial wus a farce. Old Mochan got up and did his bit, right enough. He stuck his neck right out and told them the whole story – detail by detail, as he had seen it wae his own eyes. It wus obvious he was telling the truth but that didnae make much difference. **(Smiles again. Judge's voice.)** You must make up your minds on the credibility and reliability of the evidence you have heard. The matter of the verdict, credibility and reliability, which facts are proved, and which not, are matters for you alone . . .

BYRNE smiles. Next part is done with off-stage voices.

VOICES: What is your verdict?

The verdict is Guilty.

Is that verdict unanimous or by a majority?

It is by a majority.

BYRNE: My lawyer passed me a note. It said 'You didn't stand a chance. It was either you or three married men. They didn't dare do otherwise.' After that I went on yet another journey.

Enter three screws. They lay hands on BYRBE, handcuffing him. They push him into centre stage and begin to construct the cage around him. PAISLEY punctuates the making of the cage with the speech of the prosecuting advocate, which he delivers with great relish.

PAISLEY: My Lord, I move for sentence. The Accused is 24 years of age and I produce a Schedule of previous convictions, and your Lordship will see that there have been **(fifteen)** previous convictions dating from when the accused was a juvenile. The initial convictions are of offences of dishonesty. In particular, in 1963, he was sentenced to two years imprisonment for assault to severe injury and assault by stabbing . . . February 1963, sentenced to imprisonment for assaulting the police and attempting to resist arrest. Two years imprisonment in 1965 for assault and again in October 1965. 1967 sentenced to life imprisonment for murder. 1968 another 18 months for assaulting the assistant governor of one of Her Majesty's prisons, and now, here's a wee hit more for you. Tell him, Renfrew!

RENFREW: **(Also taking off Judge.)** John Byrne. You have a deplorable record and you are now serving a sentence of life imprisonment for murder. **(Loud send-up 'tut tuts' from PAISLEY and RENFREW.)** I cannot emphasise too much that if you are to serve your sentence of imprisonment in such a way as to obtain some remission, you must behave yourself. **(PAISLEY and RENFREW nod sagely at this.)**

PAISLEY: Did you hear that, Johnny? Behave yourself.

RENFREW: The sentence I am about to pronounce will have some effect – **(laughing in his own voice.)** you bet your fucking life it'll have some effect – **(Judge's voice again.)** some effect in that it will be taken into consideration if and when you are released, when the time comes for consideration **(own voice)** but only consideration – of your release. I now sentence you to ha ha ha four years' imprisonment.

PAISLEY: Hear that, Johnny? Another four years on top of what you've already got. If you ever get out of here, it will be in your coffin. See you later!

Exit SCREWS.

MOCHAN: John Byrne, you've gone beyond the physical wae these people. Its no your body they're trying tae break – its yir proud spirit, because that's what they really fear.

Exit MOCHAN.

Percussion, very quiet and twitchy, behind next sequence. Fluorescent light comes on. It hurts BYRNE eyes, his head. He tries to stretch up towards it. Fails. Each time he fails another light comes on. He tries to climb up the bars. Fails. Another light. He crouches, concentrates, prepares to spring. Leaps up, hands stretched out towards light. Falls back on to floor. Another light goes on. Sits with his hands over his eyes. Enter RENFREW.

RENFREW: What's this animal? Going to sleep? Sleeping's not allowed, especially not during the day. Yes, its during the day, animal. I'll bet that surprised you. Never mind. Its nice and bright in here anyway. Isn't it? Look, ah've brought a bit of food for you.

BYRNE takes his hands from his eyes and looks at food.

RENFREW: Hungry, are we, animal? Well, there you are,

Puts plate down outside of bars. BYRNE tries to reach it with his arm but it is too far away from him.

RENFREW: Oh, sorry. Can you not reach that? Wait and I'll move a wee bit closer for you.

Picks up plate and spits in food. Puts it down within BYRNES reach. BYRNE looks at RENFREW, looks back to food. Stretches his arm out slowly through the bars, staring at RENFREW who moves hack a little. Still staring at him he begins to eat the food – very deliberately – with his fingers.

BYRNE: You think you're going to break me, don't you?

RENFREW: **(Indicating patch on his eye.)** Well, you're not exactly my favourite person. Byrne, you could say that

BYRNE: Well, I've got news for you. I've got something in me that can't be broken, not by you nor by anybody else – no matter what you do to me.

RENFREW: Is that a challenge?

BYRNE: You don't need any challenging. You're going to try it anyway. And your food tastes like fucking sawdust. **(He throws it out through the bars.)**

RENFREW stands up.

RENFREW: Right. Byrne. That's just what I was waiting for. Paisley! Johnstone! **(They enter.)**

PAISLEY: What is it?

RENFREW: Look at the mess this animal's made. He's getting aggressive again.

PAISLEY: Oh well. We'll need to do something about that, won't we? Haud yir noses, boys, we're going into his smelly cage. . .

SCREWS enter cage While PAISLEY is talking, JOHNSTONE searches with his hands along top edge of Cage. RENFREW holds his nose and looks under chamber pot.

PAISLEY: So how do you like your new quarters, Byrne? This is the Cage and you're in Inverness. Lovely part of the world, Inverness. Too bad yae cannae get tae see any of it. Aye, yir nice and secure, Byrne. There's these bars, then there's the four walls round the bars — solid concrete. Then there's us . . . Awright, get your clothes off.

BYRNE: What is this?

PAISLEY: Get them off or we'll tear them off you.

BYRNE: Come on and try.

JOHNSTONE: We need to search you, Byrne. Official procedure.

BYRNE: Official procedure, my arse. **(Pointing at PAISLEY.)** It was that bastard's idea.

Starts taking his clothes off. angrily. When he has stripped BYRNE places his hands as a shield for his genitals.

PAISLEY: OK, search them too. **(Referring to clothes.)** Right, Byrne. Stand against the wall. Oh, look at him. Frightened somebody's gonnae manhandle you, ur yae? Don't worry, we don't want tae know about your disgusting body. Stand against the wall. OK Renfrew. Search him. Spread your legs, Byrne.

RENFREW searches him, looking under his armpits, between his toes, finally probing his rectum. BYRNE reacts violently to this. RENFREW gets away from him fast.

PAISLEY: Oh, look. He's sensitive.

BYRNE is looking aggressive.

PAISLEY: **(As they leave the cage.)** Ah see you've goat that dangerous look again, Byrne. Well you can save it fur later. We're no quite ready fur that yet. But we'll be back. Oh aye and ah think we'd better take your clothes. You never know what mischief he might get tae wae them, do you lads?

Takes clothes. BYRNE rushes at them but the cage is locked.

PAISLEY: Too late, Byrne. Its too late for you for anything. Your time's up. You've become one of the living dead.

BYRNE: No. So long as I'm fighting, I know that I'm alive.

PAISLEY: Aye, well ah've telt yae — we'll be back. And we're gonnae knock the fighting out of your system once and for all.

Drums. Exit SCREWS. PAISLEY pauses.

PAISLEY: Cover yourself, you disgusting bastard.

BYRNE makes V signs at PAISLEY who laughs. Drums continue. Scotland the Brave. SCREWS exit. Starts to pace the interior of the cage. Jogs on the spot. Jogs round the cage. Stops, overcome with weariness for a moment, resting his head against his arm.

Begins again, doing press-ups and other exercises. Sits down and adopts Yoga half-lotus posture. He feels the floor with the flat of his hand, then runs his hands over the bare skin of his body.

Enter CAROLE. She stands looking into the cage.

CAROLE: Hello, Johnny.

BYRNE: **(Putting his hand over his eyes. Turning his head away.)** No! No!

CAROLE: Speak to me. Johnny.

BYRNE: **(Fist clenched against his brow.)** I've got to sleep. Got to sleep.

CAROLE: You can change things, you know, Johnny.

BYRNE: Shut up! Shut up you bloody ghost.

Exit CAROLE. Enter KELLY.

KELLY: Hiya, Johnny. Dae yae like ma scar? You gave me it, Johnny. Remember?

Enter DIDI.

DIDI: Aye. Remember, Johnny? Yir Big Brass knew how tae treat yae well. But ah think you've hud yir oats just wance too often.

Enter LEWIS.

LEWIS: There might be a loophole, Johnny, a legal loophole.

CAROLE: Five year six year seven year more.

DIDI: Eight Nine Ten Eleven Twelve Thirteen . . . Whit age ur you?

KELLY: They're knockin down the Gorbals. The old place will he gone by the time you get out, If you ever get out.

DIDI: If he ever gets out of here it'll he in his coffin.

Enter PAISLEY.

PAISLEY: Aye. And we'll make sure the lid is well screwed down. **(All other characters freeze.)** We've come fur yae animal. We've come tae break yae.

BYRNE stands up.

BYRNE: Come on then.

Enter JOHNSTONE and RENFREW.

BYRNE: Ah promise yae ah'll make it as unpleasant as possible. If yir gonnae break me, yir gonnae break yersels tae. **(Laughs.)** Ah hud a dream under these bright lights, you know, that wis forty winks youse didnae know ah'd hud . . .

PAISLEY: **(To others.)** He's roon the twist. When ah came in he wus talking tae himself and staring like a lunatic.

BYRNE: Ah dreamt ah hud company. A wee fly, buzzing about the place. It came down and landed on ma arm and flew away again So ah chased after it and ah caught it. Ah watched it buzzing in ma hand for a minit, then a dropt it intae that chanty there. Right intae aw the piss and shit that's all ah've goat left tae show fur ma life. And ah watched it struggle and swim about. Then ah spat oan it. It wus in real trouble then, flailing about. Ah said, Hello there, wee brother. Ah know exactly how you feel. And Ah watched it struggle towards a large lump of shit and crawl up on it for refuge. A moment later ah wus wakened by more of your banging and thumping. And ah could smell your stinking bodies and your smelly feet all the way through those concrete walls. Ah could hear you talking. Ah ran ma hands over ma body and it felt sharp and strong. Ah felt ma own skin and it amazed me. Ah touched the floor. It was so alive, **(so there)**. Ah could feel every speck of dust. And when ah looked down, the dust was like jewels, when ah breathed, the air was like nectar. It was strange. Ah felt happy. Ah felt happier than I'd ever felt in my life before. Happy. And grateful. Grateful just to be standing here, breathing in the stinking air. Alive. And ah thought. If that shit could help the fly, it can help me too. **(He cakes his body in shit from the chamberpot.)** So come on. Come on and get me. **(Smears over his face.)** How much of it can you accept?

During this speech the SCREWS have drawn out their batons. At the end of the speech they have their batons held up menacingly and BYRNE stands facing them. At the ready. The lights go down slowly. As they go down, the various characters exit slowly taking

off their costumes. The words are delivered wearily and sadly as they exit.

RENFREW: Rats.

JOHNSTONE: Rats aroon the back.

CAROLE: Rats aroon the back an a wee dug.

PAISLEY: Rats aroon the back an a wee dug that wus rerr ut breakin their necks.

RENFREW: It kilt that many rats it goat a mention in the papers.

CAROLE: It broke that many necks, it goat a medal fur it.

BYRNE: **(Lights are almost out.)** My name is Byrne. Johnny Byrne. This is my version of my story.

The End